# WORLD TRADE

## Toward Fair and Free Trade in the Twenty-first Century

*Edited by*
Jo Marie Griesgraber and Bernhard G. Gunter

Pluto Press
LONDON • CHICAGO, IL.
with
Center of Concern Washington, DC

First published 1997 by Pluto Press
345 Archway Road, London N6 5AA
and 1436 West Randolph, Chicago, Illinois 60607, USA



British Library Cataloguing in Publication Data
A catalogue record for this book is available from the British Library.

ISBN 0 7453 1054 0 hbk

Library of Congress Cataloging-in-Publication Data
World trade: toward a fair and free trade in the twenty-first century / edited by Jo Marie Griesgraber and Bernhard G. Gunter.
p. cm. — (Rethinking Bretton Woods : v. 5)
Includes bibliographical references and index.
ISBN 0–7483–1054–0
1. International trade. 2. International finance. 3. Twenty-first century—Forecasts. I. Griesgraber, Jo Marie. II. Gunter, Bernhard G. 1965– . III. Series.
[(HF1379)]
382—dc20

96–34394
CIP

Designed, typeset and produced for Pluto Press by
Chase Production Services, Chadlington, OX7 3LN
Printed in the EC by J.W. Arrowsmith Ltd, Bristol, England

**World Trade**

**RETHINKING BRETTON WOODS**

*Series Editors:*
Jo Marie Griesgraber and Bernhard G. Gunter

This series of five books explores a broad range of proposals for achieving more equitable, sustainable and participatory development, particularly through the international financial institutions. The task of the series is to offer the activist and political communities insights into effecting genuine institutional reform over the next 10 to 15 years.

**Volume I**
PROMOTING DEVELOPMENT
Effective Global Institutions for the Twenty-first Century

**Volume II**
DEVELOPMENT
New Paradigms and Principles for the Twenty-first Century

**Volume III**
THE WORLD BANK
Lending on a Global Scale

**Volume IV**
THE WORLD'S MONETARY SYSTEM
Toward Stability and Sustainability in the Twenty-first Century

**Volume V**
WORLD TRADE
Toward Fair and Free Trade in the Twenty-first Century

# Contents

## LIST OF FIGURES



## LIST OF TABLES

This volume is dedicated to
CHAKRAVARTHI RAGHAVAN,
Chief Editor of the
South–North Development Monitor – SUNS.

# Preface

To explore a broad range of proposals for achieving more equitable, sustainable and participatory development, particularly through the international financial institutions, the Center of Concern convened a conference in Washington, DC, from 12–17 June, 1994. The conference was a part of the Rethinking Bretton Woods project, which marked the fiftieth anniversary of the Bretton Woods, New Hampshire, meeting that created the World Bank and the International Monetary Fund (IMF) and laid the groundwork for the General Agreement on Tariffs and Trade (GATT), succeeded by the World Trade Organization (WTO) in 1995.

Conference participants came from 27 countries in Africa, Asia, Australia, Europe, and North and South America, and included economists, historians, sociologists, lawyers, businesspeople, political scientists, theologians and representatives of the Bretton Woods institutions (BWIs). Their papers and discussions focused on roles for the BWIs – the World Bank, the IMF and the soon-to-be-established WTO – in initiating, assisting and sustaining such development. This series of books originated as the preparatory papers for that conference.

The project's 23 sponsors include people from academic and non-governmental institutions in 18 countries; an advisory group has members from nine countries. The lead organization, the Center of Concern, is a Washington DC-based social justice center founded in 1971 to analyze, educate and advocate on issues of international development. Louis Goodman, Dean of the School of International Service at The American University, a project adviser and co-sponsor, hosted the conference.

This book is the result of the hard work and generosity of many: the advisers and sponsors of Rethinking Bretton Woods; the funders, the John D. and Catherine T. MacArthur Foundation, the Ford Foundation, the C.S. Mott Foundation, the World Council of Churches, CEBEMO, Trocaire and CAFOD, and their very competent staffs; the staff and interns of the Center of

Concern; the style editors Jane Deren, Renee Y. Storteboom, Marie Walters and Elena McCollim and the staff at Pluto Press, Roger van Zwanenberg, Robert Webb, et al., and Jeanne Brady, editor at Cove Publishing Support Services. The editors appreciate deeply the support and good humor of families: Shaw, Andrea, Stanley, David and Jesmin.

Jo Marie Griesgraber
Bernhard G. Gunter
Washington, DC
October 1995

# List of Acronyms

| | |
|---|---|
| AFL-CIO | American Federation of Labor and Congress of Industrial Organizations |
| BIS | Bank for International Settlement |
| BWI | Bretton Woods institution |
| DSB | Dispute Settlement Body |
| DSU | Dispute Settlement Understanding |
| EBRD | European Bank for Reconstruction and Development |
| ECOSOC | Economic and Social Council |
| EC | European Community |
| ERP | effective rates of protection |
| FAO | Food and Agriculture Organization |
| FDI | foreign direct investment |
| Fed | US Federal Reserve Board |
| G-7 | Group of Seven |
| G-24 | Group of Twenty-Four |
| GATS | General Agreement on Trade in Services |
| GATT | General Agreement on Tariffs and Trade |
| GDP | Gross Domestic Product |
| GNP | Gross National Product |
| GSP | Generalized System of Preferences |
| HDI | Human Development Index |
| IBRD | International Bank for Reconstruction and Development |
| ICCR | Interfaith Center for Corporate Responsibility |
| ICFTU | International Confederation of Free Trade Unions |
| IDA | International Development Association |
| IDB | Inter-American Development Bank |
| IFC | International Finance Corporation |
| IFI | international financial institution |
| IMF | International Monetary Fund |
| ILO | International Labour Organisation |
| IPA | Indian Patents Act |
| ITC | International Trade Commission |

| | |
|---|---|
| ITO | International Trade Organization |
| KRRS | Karnataka Rajya Rayat Sangh |
| MDB | multilateral development bank |
| MFA | Multi-Fibre Arrangement |
| MFN | most favored nation |
| MIGA | Multilateral Investment Guarantee Agency |
| MTN | Multilateral Trade Negotiation |
| NAFTA | North American Free Trade Agreement |
| NGO | non-governmental organization |
| NIC | newly industrialized country |
| OECD | Organization for Economic Cooperation and Development |
| PMP | Phased Manufacturing Program |
| PUDR | People's Union for Democratic Rights (India) |
| R&D | research and development |
| SAP | structural adjustment program |
| SDR | special drawing right |
| TNC | transnational corporation |
| TRIMs | Trade-Related Investment Measures |
| TRIPs | Trade-Related Intellectual Property Rights |
| UNCTAD | United Nations Conference on Trade and Development |
| UNDP | United Nations Development Programme |
| UNEP | United Nations Environment Programme |
| UNESCO | United Nations Educational, Scientific and Cultural Organization |
| UNICEF | United Nations International Children's Emergency Fund |
| VER | voluntary export restraint |
| WFP | World Food Programme |
| WHO | World Health Organization |
| WIPO | World Intellectual Property Organization |
| WTO | World Trade Organization |

# Introduction

A brief historical overview of trade theories and of the General Agreement for Tariffs and Trade (GATT) provides the context for the wide-ranging and profound discussions of trade which constitute the chapters in this volume. Earlier volumes in this series considered practical reforms of the World Bank and the International Monetary Fund (IMF) toward effective global institutions (Volume I); alternative principles and paradigms for development (Volume II); and in-depth explorations of the history and potential roles for the World Bank and the IMF (Volumes III and IV, respectively). It is appropriate that the newest global financial institution, the World Trade Organization (WTO), which was conceived at Bretton Woods, should be the focus of this fifth and final volume of the Rethinking Bretton Woods Series.

## A BRIEF HISTORY OF TRADE THEORIES

Although trade theory has gone through distinct periods, economic theory generally suggests there are gains from international trade even for developing countries. In theory, increased trade fosters rapid growth of employment and a more equitable distribution of income. The practice of international trade often contradicted that theory. While free trade certainly enforced efficiency, the gains from trade and higher efficiency have generally not been distributed equally. This has been true not only within countries but also among countries. Dependence on international trade with its unequal distribution of benefits led the so-called dependency theorists of the 1960s and 1970s (like Paul Baran and Andre Gunder Frank) to conclude that international trade led to exploitation and neocolonialism: 'According to Frank, a developing country can develop only by withdrawing from the world capitalist system.'[1] Frank's prescriptions are now rejected even by former populist economists as being unrealistic for developing countries.

Trade theory has evolved considerably since the mercantilists (1500–1750) saw international trade as a zero-sum game. That is, one country's gain was automatically another country's loss. According to mercantilist theory, countries with a trade surplus gained at the expense of countries with a trade deficit. Adam Smith (1723–1790) substituted the mercantilists' zero-sum approach to trade with the concept of absolute advantage, showing that it was possible to gain from international trade even in the case of a trade deficit.[2]

David Ricardo (1772–1823) substantially corrected the concept of absolute advantage by introducing the concept of comparative advantage.[3] Contemporary economists Eli Heckscher and Bertil Ohlin modified the concept of comparative advantage by basing it on different factor endowments among countries. They demonstrated that the more different countries were in their endowments, the higher would be the gains of trade between the countries. Based on comparative advantages, free trade was the 'first-best' policy from a theoretical point of view. However, there were practical problems with free trade. Within any country, some groups gain while other groups lose. Although the overall gains were supposed to be larger than the losses, the problem of a fair distribution of benefits endures.

Only in 1979 did trade theory begin to catch up with the practice of protectionism. That year Paul Krugman[4] demonstrated that free trade was not necessarily the first-best solution due either to increasing returns to scale[5] or to externalities (or 'spillovers'), which are the main elements of the so-called 'new trade theories'. Based on increasing returns to scale or positive externalities, the models of the new trade theories illustrate that a country could gain either by protectionist measures or by export promotion policies. However, these gains are not mutual – one country's gain is another country's loss. Although free trade may still be the overall optimal solution, free trade is no longer the first-best solution from the individual country's point of view. Protectionism and unfair trade practices, long practiced widely, could finally be justified theoretically. The possibility that one country could gain at the cost of another intensified the call for extending the international economic order to the international trading system. This was the state of theory and practice when the latest round of GATT negotiations began in earnest. To understand the hopes and misgivings surrounding the establishment of the WTO, it is useful to review some of the history leading up to its creation.

## A BRIEF HISTORY OF THE GATT

Efforts to include trade issues within the rules of the international economic order have abounded at least since the 1944 Bretton Woods conference, which envisaged the International Trade Organization (ITO) as the third pillar of the international order (the other two being the World Bank and the International Monetary Fund, created at that same conference). As Hans Singer pointed out in Volume I of this series, 'Keynes, like the other participants, left Bretton Woods in the firm belief that the ITO would be established.'[6] The negotiations on the ITO were completed on 24 March 1948 with the signing of the Final Act (also called the Havana Charter) of the United Nations Conference on Trade and Employment (November 1947–March 1948) in Havana, Cuba. Months earlier, 23 countries of the Geneva Trade Conference of October 1947 had already adopted a single document called the General Agreement on Tariffs and Trade (GATT). The GATT entered into effect January 1, 1948 as an interim agreement, pending the creation of the ITO as the permanent UN trade agency. Since the Havana Charter – and thus the ITO – was never ratified, the GATT became *de facto* the multilateral organization for trade-related issues.

The GATT lacked the jurisdiction and continuity of a permanent institution, being little more than a framework for successive multilateral trade negotiations. Following the Geneva Trade Conference of October 1947 there have been seven major GATT conferences or negotiation sessions:

- the Conference of Annecy, France (1949),
- the Conference of Torquay, United Kingdom (1950),
- the Conference of Geneva (1956),
- the Dillon Round (1962),
- the Kennedy Round (1964–67),
- the Tokyo Round (1973–79), and finally
- the Uruguay Round (1986–94).

The GATT has generally been considered a success in reducing tariffs and increasing trade volumes around the world:

> The value of world merchandise trade reached an all-time high of over $3.7 trillion in 1992 [... whereby ...] the industrialized countries dominate world trade, accounting for about 70 percent of world trade in recent years. ... [T]rade in manufacturers accounts for over 70 percent of international trade, with the remaining amount consisting of primary products.[7]

The Uruguay Round was launched in September 1986 in Punta del Este, Uruguay and concluded on April 15, 1994 at Marrakesh, Morocco. Although the WTO that emerged at Marrakesh lacks the ITO's essential functions in the area of commodity price stabilization, it is the widest-ranging multilateral trade agreement ever negotiated. The following 28 agreements, taken together, constitute the establishment of the WTO:[8]

I. Multilateral Agreement on Trade in Goods

1. GATT 1994 (a total of 8 agreements with modifications of the original GATT)
2. Agreement on Agriculture
3. Agreement on the Application of Sanitary and Phytosanitary Measures
4. Agreement on Textiles and Clothing
5. Agreement on Technical Barriers to Trade
6. Agreement on Trade-Related Investment Measures (TRIMs)
7. Agreement on the Implementation of Article VI of the GATT 1994 (anti-dumping)
8. Agreement on the Implementation of Article VII of the GATT 1994 (customs valuation)
9. Agreement on Preshipment Inspection
10. Agreement on Rules of Origin
11. Agreement on Import Licensing Procedures
12. Agreement on Subsidies and Countervailing Measures
13. Agreement on Safeguards

II. General Agreement on Trade in Services (GATS)

III. Agreement on Trade-Related Aspects of Intellectual Property Rights (TRIPs)

IV. Understanding on Rules and Procedures Governing the Settlement of Disputes (DSU)

V. Trade Policy Review Mechanism (TPRM)

VI. Plurilateral Trade Agreements

1. Agreement on Trade in Civil Aircraft
2. Agreement on Government Procurement
3. International Dairy Agreement
4. International Bovine Meat Agreement

It is not yet clear whether the results of the Uruguay Round represent, on balance, a positive or negative set of trade arrangements for the developing countries. While extensive studies by World Bank economists draw a generally positive picture of the impact of the Uruguay Round on developing countries,[9] Agosin, Tussie and Crespi[10] argue that the results of the Uruguay Round will harm the trade prospects for developing countries. Dani Rodrik of Columbia University is slightly more optimistic and identifies important ways in which the Uruguay Round agreements promise to strengthen multilateral discipline in world trade, which, in itself, could be beneficial for developing countries.[11] He argues that the real threats to developing countries reside in the post-Uruguay agenda, particularly in the demands for upward harmonization in the areas of labor and environment. Ann Weston, Program Director for Trade and Adjustment at the North–South Institute, Ottawa, Canada, reviewed the results of the Uruguay Round from the viewpoint of the least developed and low-income countries. She concludes that gains from the Uruguay Round will be unevenly distributed between developed and developing countries. She also stresses that '[d]eveloping countries need to take advantage of the opportunities in the ongoing post-Uruguay Round negotiations to press for changes of particular interest to them':[12]

> What is especially notable [in respect to the commodity composition of world trade] is the current importance of trade in manufactures and the declining importance of primary products. This is of particular relevance to the developing countries, whose trade has traditionally been concentrated in primary goods. ... The demand for primary products not only tends to be less responsive to income growth, but is also more likely to demonstrate greater price fluctuations. ... The lagging growth in primary goods coupled with the relative decline in primary goods prices through the middle 1980s contributed to developing countries' trade and debt problems.[13]

## DISCUSSIONS OF CONTEMPORARY TRADE ISSUES AND SOLUTIONS

With this as background let us turn now to the trade discussions here, with the emphasis on key trade issues for post-Uruguay negotiations. Chapter 1 provides in-depth information on the negotiation processes leading up to the conclusion of the GATT Uruguay Round. Specifically, it provides unique and close-up insights into the negotiations preceding the creation of the WTO. The author, Chakravarthi Raghavan, a noted journalist based in Geneva, has produced a daily newsletter, *South-North Development Monitor SUNS*, documenting trade negotiations since 1980. Raghavan interprets the significance of several of these negotiated points for the South. He analyzes the implications of the WTO for the perpetuation of an already asymmetric international trading system. Along with many analysts from the South, he expresses concern about new forms of protectionism from the North, under a guise of concern for the environment or labor rights. Raghavan concludes with issues discussed in Volume IV of this series, *The World's Monetary System: Toward Stability and Sustainability in the Twenty-first Century*, namely, the complementary changes in monetary and exchange-rate policies which are necessary to create a stable world order.

In Chapter 2, Stephen Sleigh, currently Director of Strategic Resources for the International Association of Machinists and Aerospace Workers, analyzes trade by looking at the impact of the North American Free Trade Agreement (NAFTA) and the WTO on workers in industrialized countries. In contrast with Raghavan, he suggests attaching labor rights and standards to trade agreements and offers the economic and social rationale for doing so, to the benefit of workers in both industrialized and developing countries. Sleigh first examines the employment and distributional effects of NAFTA. He goes on to explore the example of the European Community's response to the social dimensions of creating the European Union. Sleigh concludes his study with a proposal for a new approach to deal with the social dimensions of North American integration.

Chapter 3 focuses on India, where Professor Bernard D'Mello of the Management Development Institute in Gurgaon, India, outlines how India has adjusted structurally since 1973. D'Mello interprets what he finds as 'neo-imperialism', which has reproduced mass poverty and inequality. D'Mello seeks to interpret recent social and economic phenomena by looking at the rules and priorities common to the Uruguay Round, the World Bank and the IMF. He analyzes how the WTO works in concert with the Bank and the Fund in managing the international trade and payments mechanism. D'Mello argues that India is basically in transition from degenerated national capitalism to neoliberal, peripheral capitalism, which is leading to deepening under-development.

Chapter 4 reflects the experiences of Tissa Balasuriya, OMI, a Catholic priest working with Sri Lanka's poor and advocating for them among the country's intellectual and political elite. Balasuriya describes Sri Lanka's experiences with what he calls 'neoliberal policies' and trade liberalizations. His analysis shows not only that Sri Lanka's economic situation has deteriorated in many aspects, especially for the poor, but also carries a forceful critique of the World Bank's structural adjustment programs (SAPs) and the growing power of transnational corporations (TNCs). He concludes not with a call for isolation or withdrawal from the market, but with a call for an informed national dialogue in which affected people have a voice in deciding their future, while economic and political leaders are challenged to bring social and moral consciousness to their policy work. Balasuriya's critique of the TNCs provides a useful introduction to the final chapter.

John Cavanagh, a senior fellow at the Institute for Policy Studies in Washington, DC, and at the Transnational Institute in Amsterdam, is the rare person able to straddle the debate laid out in Chapters 1 and 2, that is, whether labor, environmental and human rights conditions are appropriate to the WTO and other trade instruments (being among the few international instruments that have enforcement powers), or whether such 'social conditions' are merely the most recent incarnation of protectionism in the North against imports from the developing countries of the South. In Chapter 5, Cavanagh brings his expertise on transnational corporations to the debate. Having just co-authored *Global Dreams: Imperial Corporations and the New World Order*[14] with Richard Barnet, Cavanagh's broad yet detailed knowledge of TNCs is evident as he explores their role in the global economy. This contribution is essential to any discussion of global trade, for the TNCs are the most numerous and powerful actors in global trade, frequently dwarfing the nation states that negotiated the trade framework for the WTO. Cavanagh offers proposals for regulating TNCs to make them socially accountable. First, he describes the need for and concept of accountability. He then assesses the possibility of corporate accountability through trade agreements. He closes the chapter, the book and the series by proposing steps to move forward with corporate accountability.

## NOTES

1. W. Wayne Nafziger, *The Economics of Developing Countries*, 2nd ed. (Englewood Cliffs, NJ: Prentice Hall, 1990) p. 93.
2. Adam Smith, *An Inquiry Into the Nature and Causes of the Wealth of Nations* (London: W. Strahn and T. Cadwell, 1776; reprinted London: J.M. Dent and Sons, 1977).
3. David Ricardo, 'On the Principles of Political Economy, and Taxation' (London: John Murray, 1817) as reprinted in Piero Sraffa (ed.) with the collaboration of M.H. Dobb, *The Works and Correspondence of David Ricardo*, Vol. I (Cambridge, England: University Press for the Royal Economic Society, 1951).
4. Paul R. Krugman, 'Increasing Returns, Monopolistic Competition and International Trade' *Journal of International Economics*, vol. 9/4 (November 1979) pp. 467–79; and Paul R. Krugman, 'A Model of Innovation, Technological Transfer, and the World Distribution of Income', *Journal of Political Economy*, vol. 87/2 (April 1979) pp. 253–66.
5. Returns to scale is 'the rate at which output changes as the quantities of all inputs are varied ... This should be carefully distinguished from the situation in which only one input is varied in which case the law of diminishing returns will eventually come into play': David W. Pearce (ed.), *The MIT Dictionary of Modern Economics*, 4th ed. (Cambridge, Mass.: The MIT Press, 1992) p. 376.
6. Hans W. Singer, 'Rethinking Bretton Woods: From an Historical Perspective' in Jo Marie Griesgraber and Bernhard G. Gunter (eds) *Promoting Development: Effective Global Institutions for the Twenty-first Century* (London: Pluto Press with Center of Concern, 1995) p. 8.
7. Dennis R. Appleyard and Alfred J. Field, *International Economics*, 2nd ed. (Chicago et al: Irwin, 1995) pp. 4–7.
8. See Box 1 of Dani Rodrik, 'Developing Countries after the Uruguay Round', in United Nations Conference on Trade and Development (UNCTAD), *International Monetary and Financial Issues for the 1990s*, Research Papers for the Group of Twenty-Four (New York and Geneva: United Nations, 1995) p. 40.
9. See for example, Bernard M. Hoekman, 'Trade Laws and Institutions: Good Practices and the World Trade Organization', *World Bank Discussion Papers*, no. 282 (Washington, DC: World Bank, 1995); and Will Martin and L. Alan Winters (eds), 'The Uruguay Round and the Developing Economies', *World Bank Discussion Papers*, no. 307 (Washington, DC: World Bank, 1995).

10. Manuel R. Agosin, Diana Tussie and Gustavo Crespi, 'Developing Countries and the Uruguay Round: An Evaluation and Issues for the Future' in United Nations Conference on Trade and Development (UNCTAD), *International Monetary and Financial Issues for the 1990s*, Research Papers for the Group of Twenty-Four (New York and Geneva: United Nations, 1995) pp. 1–34.
11. Dani Rodrik, 'Developing Countries after the Uruguay Round', in United Nations Conference on Trade and Development (UNCTAD), *International Monetary and Financial Issues for the 1990s*, Research Papers for the Group of Twenty-Four (New York and Geneva: United Nations, 1995) pp. 35–60.
12. Ann Weston, 'The Uruguay Round: Unravelling the Implications for the Least Developed and Low-Income Countries' in United Nations Conference on Trade and Development (UNCTAD), *International Monetary and Financial Issues for the 1990s*, Research Papers for the Group of Twenty-Four (New York and Geneva: United Nations, 1995) p. 95.
13. Dennis R. Appleyard and Alfred J. Field, *International Economics*, 2nd ed. (Chicago: Irwin, 1995) p. 7.
14. Richard J. Barnet and John Cavanagh, *Global Dreams: Imperial Corporations and the New World Order* (New York: Simon & Schuster, 1994).

# 1 A New Trade Order in a World of Disorder?

*Chakravarthi Raghavan*

## INTRODUCTION

Fifty years ago, the political, economic and social world order was envisioned as a whole. The UN Charter and its specialized organs were all part of this vision of a new world order. The Economic and Social Council (ECOSOC) was given the coordinating role in the economic and social field over the entire UN system and specialized agencies. Although the Bretton Woods institutions (BWIs) were founded before the United Nations they were not envisaged in their present role whereby they are formulating and pushing their own economic and development policies, usurping the Charter role of the United Nations and ECOSOC.

Most of what is known as the Third World or the South had no hand in the fashioning of the BWIs nor the post-war vision underlying them nor the United Nations. It was the effort of the United States and Britain – with some commonality of vision and many differences too – into which others were brought in, but without any real effective say. On the US side, in the very beginning, President Roosevelt spoke of freedom for all; but on the British side, Winston Churchill had rejected it. After Roosevelt's death, with President Truman's entrance into the White House, the views about colonies became even more muted. Though the United States was determined to end the British imperial preferences and the like, as the work on the BWIs and later the Havana Charter for an International Trade Organization (ITO) progressed, the independence of the colonies and their charting of their own course figured little or not at all.

The Bretton Woods system of fixed exchange rates collapsed in 1971 – when President Nixon repudiated the US guarantee of exchanging \$35 for an ounce of gold; it was replaced by the floating exchange-rate system. The International Monetary Fund

(IMF) lost a crucial part of its legitimacy at that point. Though the IMF holds periodic Article IV consultations with all its members, it has no influence whatsoever over the major industrial countries, nor has the World Bank. After 1973, both have been attempting to ensure that the policies agreed upon by the major industrial countries are carried out by the South. They 'function not merely as lenders of last resort but virtually as instruments of neo-colonial governance on behalf of their OECD shareholders'.[1]

The Third World has come under the grip of the BWIs' philosophy and their structural adjustment programs (SAPs). The BWIs' philosophy is a fundamentalist ideology of the market that is not even practiced in the industrialized countries. The results of the SAPs are now seen as mixed or, in the case of Africa, as a failure.[2] Since 1991, the sway of the BWIs has extended over Eastern Europe and the former Soviet Union.

The BWIs' record is far from the claim of success that their glossily printed studies and publications or their well-financed publicity apparatus make it out to be. Political and social upheavals, often bordering on chaos, cannot be disassociated from the BWIs' policies thrust upon developing countries. All that the two institutions are able to claim now is that things would have been worse without their policies! With its large resources, its influence on other international financial institutions (IFIs) and its practical unaccountability to anyone, the World Bank has in fact established the most dangerous monopoly of all – a near-monopoly of research.[3]

The Charter for an ITO (also called the Havana Charter) was adopted by the United Nations Conference on Trade and Employment held in Havana, Cuba during November 1947–March 1948. That Charter proposed the International Trade Organization (ITO), seen as working closely with the IMF. Moreover, the ITO was conceived as part of the UN system, given its much wider role.

The General Agreement on Tariffs and Trade (GATT), put in place under a protocol of provisional application as a temporary arrangement of 23 Contracting Parties at the Geneva Trade Conference of 1947, pending the entry into force of the Havana Charter and the ITO envisaged therein, had no organizational provision. The GATT Secretariat came into being under the Interim Committee for the ITO that the United Nations set up in 1948 pending establishment of the ITO under the Havana Charter. Thereafter, GATT members, also called Contracting Parties, made decisions relating to the GATT Secretariat from time to time, but never formally established one. All along, the Contracting Parties saw the GATT Secretariat as one purely to service the General Agreement and nothing more.

For a while, after the GATT was set up in 1947, and till the late 1950s, there had been the hope that the United States could be persuaded to ratify the Havana Charter and thus the ITO could be established. But by the late 1950s, it became clear that the Havana Charter was dead. The industrial countries were quite comfortable with the GATT as a provisional treaty and a contract among governments.

## FROM THE GATT TO THE WORLD TRADE ORGANIZATION (WTO)

### *Concerns of Developing Countries*

By the early 1960s, the developing countries saw the international economic system as not supportive of their development. The half-hearted attempts in the GATT to deal with developing countries' problems, as taken up in the Haberler Committee report,[4] for example, did not lead to much.

Developing countries then spearheaded a drive that led to the establishment in 1964 of the UN Conference on Trade and Development (UNCTAD) as a UN General Assembly organ in 1964. The GATT tried unsuccessfully to head it off through an amendment – Part IV of its General Agreement – providing special treatment for developing countries. The amendment called for, among other things:

- special measures to improve market access for developing countries on a non-reciprocal basis,
- refraining from raising tariff barriers, and
- fiscal measures affecting developing country exports.

But all of these were on 'best endeavor basis' and were not implemented in practice. Not only were no special benefits provided but special discriminatory measures were put in place against them. At UNCTAD quadrennial conferences, the idea of the ITO was talked about, but not at the GATT. The establishment of an ITO or any other trade organization is not among the subjects listed in any part of the Punta del Este Declaration[5] in

September 1986, which marked the beginning of the GATT's Uruguay Round of Multilateral Trade Negotiations.

### *The GATT Secretariat's Agenda*

However, the anomaly of the GATT Secretariat attaining legitimacy only via the Interim Committee for the ITO had irked the GATT Secretariat for quite some time. The establishment of a trade organization through the Uruguay Round – finding an institutional basis for the secretariat and making the new organization an equal partner with the IMF and the World Bank in the international economic arena, particularly in the supervision and running of developing countries' trade policies[6] – had always been part of the hidden agenda of the GATT Secretariat and Arthur Dunkel, Director-General from 1980 until July 1993.

The Punta del Este mandate, Part I.E. 'Functioning of the GATT System' envisaged the Uruguay Round negotiations as:

- enhancing surveillance of the GATT in trade policies and practices of the Contracting Parties and its effects on the multilateral trading system,

- improving the overall effectiveness of the GATT's decision-making through measures like the involvement of Ministers, and

- increasing the GATT's contribution to coherence in global economic policymaking.

This was at best an incidental negotiating issue that acquired a momentum of its own, thanks to the institutional loyalties of some ambassadors accredited to the GATT who saw its usefulness to enhance their own status back home. The Secretariat maneuvered to have a separate negotiating group set up for the functioning of the GATT system. But the idea of a post-Uruguay Round trade organization did not even surface in the early discussions of this negotiating group.[7] Even more, neither the European Community nor the United States (which was primarily responsible for pushing these negotiations since 1981) had the establishment of an international trade organization in mind. Neither in the discussions at the GATT during the preparatory process (1984–86) nor in the US congressional discussions (before or after Punta del Este) is there any reference to the idea of an international trade organization.

While the negotiations were launched in 1986, it was only in 1988 that the US Congress granted the President authority to negotiate – the 'fast-track authority' under which Congress undertakes to consider and dispose of any trade agreement with a 'yes' or 'no' vote, without making any amendments. There are references in the congressional discussions over the Omnibus Trade and Competitiveness Act of 1988 about improving the functioning of the GATT and its dispute settlement system, but no mention of an organization. Given the long-standing US congressional opposition to give up its authority over trade policy (which was the main reason why Congress did not want to ratify the Havana Charter), it is doubtful whether any fast-track authority would have been granted by the US Congress if there had been any such idea.

At Punta del Este, and in the two years of preparations preceding the launch of the negotiations, the Contracting Parties (whether from the North or the South) had no institutional issues in mind. The governments were concerned with the substantive issues.[8] However, the institutional agenda was quietly pushed in the negotiations of the 'Functioning of the GATT System' by the Secretariat, with the help of a few negotiators who mostly acted without authority from their governments – first in terms of GATT/IMF/World Bank collaboration, and later in 1990 as just a common house for all the separate agreements and a way of establishing a Secretariat.

### *The European Community's Support*

In the negotiating group on GATT articles, the European Community had asked for a review of the GATT Protocol of Provisional Application, with a view to ending the US 'grandfather clause' privileges,[9] which the European Community and many others complained had been abused. In the negotiating group on Dispute Settlement, the European Community and others brought up a proposal (which they wanted to get adopted as part of the mid-term review package of the Uruguay Round) that Contracting Parties be committed to adjust and/or administer their domestic trade policy laws and enforcement procedures in a manner ensuring conformity of all measures with the GATT dispute settlement procedures and decisions. This would have effectively put an end to all the Section 301 laws.[10] But at the mid-term review, the United States had made clear its opposition – on the grounds that the US Congress would not agree to it. The European Community gave up the idea and began looking for other ways to deal with it.

With GATT functioning as a provisional treaty and in virtual non-transparency, and as a contract among governments, GATT representatives have always prided themselves on their free-wheeling ways of negotiating and concluding accords that are difficult under formal international treaty-making processes. Throughout the negotiations, the negotiating mandate was constantly changed informally. So much so, that in 1990 an EC negotiator in another context blandly told the press that in GATT 'anything is possible between consenting adults'.[11]

In the run-up to the mid-term review at Montreal in December 1988, the idea surfaced that GATT, IMF and World Bank act together and that GATT's Director-General be given a free hand in this. This was quickly killed by the developing countries who did not want to have another 'old man of the sea' on their backs. Even the GATT Director-General's mandate to talk to the heads of the IMF and the World Bank (and report back to the Contracting Parties) was circumscribed.

However, the Secretariat did not abandon its ambitions. The European Community first spoke in December 1989 of converting the GATT into an ITO. Again the European Community quickly backed off because of opposition from the developing countries who wanted to keep open the possibility of a comprehensive ITO, as envisaged in the Havana Charter, and did not want the ITO's emasculation via the GATT.

### *From Multilateral Trade Organization (MTO) to WTO*

The moves for an institutional arrangement surfaced again in 1990, with the European Community speaking of a Multilateral Trade Organization (MTO) at informal consultations chaired by the GATT Director-General Arthur Dunkel. The Italian Trade Minister Renato Ruggiero (Director-General of the WTO since May 1995) espoused an MTO in public and suggested that the topic would be one way of masking the likely failure of the Round![12]

The European Community then put forward a paper formally, in April 1990, outlining its ideas for enlarging the GATT and making it into a comprehensive international trade organization.[13] However, at that stage the European Community said it did not expect any negotiations on this at the negotiations on the 'Functioning of the GATT System'. Rather, this would be a matter for the Trade Negotiations Committee and for the final Ministerial meeting of the Uruguay Round.

Later, in the run-up to the Brussels Ministerial meeting (which was intended to conclude the negotiations, but failed), the European Community suggested that the Brussels meeting should make a commitment to consider establishment of an MTO after the conclusion of the negotiations. There was some discussion at Brussels among a small group of countries, but the Brussels meeting broke up in discord over the EC agricultural policy. When the negotiations resumed (at official levels) in Geneva in 1991, the issue was pursued in another small group, and surfaced finally in the draft text to the Final Act (also called the Dunkel text), tabled in December 1991, by GATT Director-General Arthur Dunkel. It continued to be discussed in 1992 and 1993 within a small group and began to be refined, as a way of ensuring that every one of the participants signed every one of the agreements.[14] However, it was never formally considered by the participants in that negotiating group as a whole, nor ever brought up in the Trade Negotiations Committee until the very end.

In December 1993, the proposal for an MTO was presented to an informal meeting of Heads of Delegations and finally adopted as part of the package. On the final day of that meeting, December 15, 1993, the United States successfully lobbied for the name of the organization to be changed from the Multilateral Trade Organization into the World Trade Organization.[15]

## THE WORLD TRADE ORGANIZATION

### *The WTO's Agreements*

The GATT's Uruguay Round of Multilateral Trade Negotiations (MTNs), launched in September 1986 at Punta del Este, Uruguay, was finally 'concluded' on April 15, 1994 at Marrakesh, Morocco, with the signing of a Final Act.[16] Attached to the Final Act was an agreement to establish the WTO and all the agreements concluded in the Round as annexes – nearly 400 pages of agreements and decisions, and some 20,000 pages of country schedules (bound tariff concessions, domestic and export subsidy reduction commitments in agriculture and initial commitments in services).

There are 28 agreements, including the General Agreement on Tariffs and Trade 1994 (GATT 1994) – which will be separate from the present GATT 1947 – and agreements in agriculture, textiles and clothing, Trade-Related Investment Measures (TRIMs), General Agreement on Trade in Services (GATS), the Agreement on Trade-Related Aspects of Intellectual Property Rights (TRIPs) and the Understanding on Rules and Procedures Governing the Settlement of Disputes (DSU).

The agreements concluded at Marrakesh, however, are incomplete in many areas and the Final Act, through various Ministerial decisions, has provided for the continuation of some negotiations, for example, in financial services, in basic telecommunications services, in maritime services, and in the movement of persons, which is one of the four modes for delivery of services. Other areas of built-in work programs and negotiations are also scattered throughout the texts.

Of the 125 countries that participated in the negotiations, seven signed only the Final Act; 97 others signed both the Final Act and the WTO – with 75 of these making the specific qualification that their signatures were subject to their country's ratification processes.

Like the Uruguay Round negotiations themselves, the overall result of the WTO is more than the sum of its individual parts. While the seven-and-a-half years of negotiations ended at Marrakesh, the WTO will set the stage for a process of perpetual negotiations![17] This is different from the situation under GATT 1947 where multilateral negotiations had to be agreed to specifically and launched periodically.

The Final Act provides for the WTO to be accepted as a whole, that is, acceptance of the WTO with all its annexed multilateral agreements and decisions. Four plurilateral agreements of a separate annex are all extensions of agreements already reached in the Tokyo Round (1973–79) and remain voluntary:

- the Agreement on Trade in Civil Aircraft,
- the Agreement on Government Procurement,
- the International Dairy Agreement, and
- the Arrangement Regarding Bovine Meat.

Unlike normal treaties, the WTO has no final provisions about the minimum number of acceptances by countries, their trade weights or geographical spreads for entry into force. But the representatives of governments at Marrakesh agreed in the Final Act on the desirability of the agreement entering into force on January 1, 1995 or as soon as possible thereafter.[18] However, much depended on the United States where Congress had to accept the WTO agreement and enact enabling legislation.

The WTO is so constructed that for some time the WTO and the accompanying GATT 1994 will coexist with GATT 1947, so that there will be two different contractual relationships: one among those who are members of the WTO and the other between each of them and those who are Contracting Parties to the GATT 1947. A transition period of two years has been envisaged (after the WTO enters into force) to enable those eligible to join the WTO as original members[19] to complete their domestic processes to become WTO members. At some point after the transition period, when all the major trading nations have acceded to the WTO, all WTO members will probably withdraw from the GATT 1947.

On the face of it, the WTO is a procedural umbrella agreement constructed to provide an institutional and organizational framework for the administration of the multilateral and plurilateral agreements concluded in the Uruguay Round.

In terms of scope and functions, according to Article III.2., the WTO 'shall provide the forum' for any negotiations among its members on multilateral trade relations in matters dealt with under the Agreements annexed to it and 'may provide a forum' for further negotiations on their multilateral trade relations. This last provision would suggest that other fora for other trade and trade-related issues are not really ruled out.

However, the main purpose of the WTO – apart from the stated view of providing an institutional setup for the trade system – is to force everyone to accept every one of the multilateral trade agreements and not be able to withdraw from any of them in the future without withdrawing from all of them. Another intention is to preempt trade questions being discussed or dealt with in any UN forum and prevent any move for a more comprehensive ITO to deal with all trade and economic issues as envisaged in the Havana Charter.

The Punta del Este Declaration of September 1986 launching the Uruguay Round of Multilateral Trade Negotiations (MTNs) had three parts:

- the Declaration for MTNs in goods was a decision of the GATT Contracting Parties, meeting at a Ministerial level Special

Session, and contained all the issues on the agenda of the Uruguay Round except services (Part I);

- the Declaration for MTNs in services which was adopted by the Ministers, meeting separately as representatives of governments (Part II), and

- the provision that Ministers would meet on the occasion of a Special Session of the Contracting Parties after the 'results of the Multilateral Trade Negotiations in all areas have been established' in order to decide on the implementation of the respective results (Part III).

The decision to have a two-track negotiation, one in goods and the other in services, with the institutional implementation of the agreements being put off till the results in all areas are settled was the result of a compromise. The compromise resolved a deadlock between the position of the United States and other OECD countries, supported by a large number of developing countries, for GATT MTNs to include not only goods but also services, and that of Brazil, India and some ten others who opposed it since the GATT dealt only with goods or products but not services. In talks between the group of countries led by Brazil and India and the European Community, the compromise was evolved and accepted by everyone at Punta del Este. Later, in April 1989, as a part of the Mid-Term agreement when it was agreed to extend the scope of the TRIPs negotiations (Part I of the Punta del Este Declaration) to encompass laying out norms and standards in intellectual property, it was agreed that this would be without prejudice to the views of participants about institutional implementation of the results of negotiations in TRIPs, 'which is to be determined by Ministers meeting on the occasion of a Special Session ... at the conclusion of the round'.[20]

*The WTO as a Single Undertaking*

The attempt to force everyone to accept all the agreements concluded in the negotiations has been justified on the ground that the Uruguay Round was a 'single undertaking'. But the 'single undertaking' concept strictly applied only to Part 1 (MTNs in Goods) of the Punta del Este Declaration:

> The launching, the conduct and the implementation of the outcome of the negotiations shall be treated as parts of a single undertaking. However, agreements reached at an early stage may be implemented on a provisional or a definitive basis by agreements prior to the formal conclusion of the negotiations. Early Agreements shall be taken into account in assessing the overall balance of the negotiations.[21]

This was made clear by the Indian representative, Ambassador Srirang P. Shukla[22] at a meeting of the Group of Negotiations on Goods when the EC Chief Delegate, Ambassador Tran Van-Thinh, tried to tie progress of negotiations in the goods area to progress in the services area on the basis of the 'globality' of the negotiations.[23] Shukla's statement was not challenged.

But, whether or not the 'single undertaking' was a legal concept applicable only to goods negotiations or a political concept applying to both goods and services, the launching, the conduct and the implementation of the outcome did not really commit any participant in the negotiations to accept it as a whole and to become a party to all the agreements. Nevertheless, towards the end of 1990, Canada, the European Community, Japan and the United States began to discuss how the developing countries could be 'persuaded' to accept the outcome as one package and not pick and choose among its various parts. Some of the members of the Cairns Group of agricultural exporters were also anxious to ensure that the European Community was not able to opt out of any agricultural agreement. There was also the view that there should be no 'fragmentation' of the GATT, as happened after the Tokyo Round when a number of agreements with their own rights and obligations applied only to signatories, resulting in a GATT system with varying levels of rights and obligations.[24]

In December 1992, after the US-EC Blair House accord on agriculture broke the overall deadlock and opened the way for conclusion of the Uruguay Round, the institutional questions again cropped up in the discussions among Canada, the European Community, Japan and the United States. At that stage the United States came out against the draft agreement on the MTO in the Dunkel text and proposed instead a protocol approach for a different arrangement – a GATT II.[25]

In opposing the US GATT-II idea and setting out the reasons why there should be an MTO in a 'non-paper' dated December 14, 1992, Canada said in these discussions that without an MTO (and all agreements annexed to it) it would not be possible to maintain the single undertaking beyond the conclusion of the Uruguay Round. Nor would it be possible to have: (a) a centralized decision making power, (b) an authority for amendment procedures and waivers, and (c) an institutional structure for the administration and management of the multilateral trading system. Canada also said that it was difficult to see how one of the United States' major objectives, cross-retaliation, could be carried out without a decision making central authority.

Furthermore, the Canadian unofficial document, pointed out:

> Establishing a Multilateral Trade Organization within the existing GATT system will enhance the status of the GATT by giving it a legal personality to deal with other organizations while, at the same time, *preventing the emergence of a trade organization within the UN system* [emphasis added].

### *The WTO as a Rule-Based System*

In the final stages of the negotiations, and after their conclusion, many of the negotiators have been repeatedly calling the WTO a rule-based multilateral trading system – perhaps in the view that by repeated assertions the WTO would acquire that characteristic. Much depends on how far the powerful trading nations would allow this development.

The talk of a 'rule-based' system should not be confused with the Anglo-Saxon concept of 'Rule of Law'. It is rule-based in that in most areas covered, there are detailed rules set down on paper. By and large (except in textiles and clothing and agriculture) the rules merely carry into the international arena what the United States or the European Community are doing; where they had differences and could not resolve them, the rules have a great deal of ambiguity; but in some other areas, particularly involving new obligations on developing countries (such as in TRIPs), the rules are specific, clear and even onerous.

The WTO's supreme governing body will be the Ministerial Conference, meeting at least every two years; between the Ministerial Conferences the General Council (with representatives of all members) operates. Under the General Council will be Councils for Trade in Goods, TRIPs and GATS. Other Committees and subordinate bodies to be established by the Ministerial Conference are also envisaged.

The WTO (Article IX) is to continue the practice of decision making by consensus followed in the GATT 1947. A footnote spells out what is meant by 'consensus' in the WTO: 'The body concerned shall be deemed to have decided by consensus on a matter submitted for its consideration, if no Member, present at the meeting when the decision is taken, formally objects to the proposed decision.' Under GATT 1947, Article XXV, decisions can be taken by simple majority of votes cast, except for waivers and amendments needing a two-thirds majority. But GATT 1947 functioned only by consensus for many reasons, including the legal uncertainties of GATT as a provisional treaty.

In the WTO, waivers would need a three-fourths majority and have to specify a termination date (unlike the example of the US agricultural waiver currently which is perpetual). However, the termination date is extendable. Unless extended by the WTO, all existing waivers will terminate two years after WTO's entry into force. Waivers of obligations covered by agreements with an implementation period (for example, agriculture obligations, TRIPs, and textiles and clothing phase-out provisions) would need consensus.

Any member of the WTO can propose an amendment to the provisions of the WTO and multilateral agreements in its Annex I by submitting a proposal to the Ministerial Conference which, for a period of 90 days from submission, has to decide by consensus, and thereafter by a two-thirds majority, on submitting the amendment to Members for acceptance.

Amendments to the WTO's provisions on Article IX (decision making), Article X (amendment provisions), Article I and Article II of GATT 1994 (most favored nation (MFN) clause and schedules of concessions), Article II.1. of GATS (MFN clause) and Article IV of TRIPs (MFN clause) can take effect only upon acceptance by all Members.

Other amendments to the WTO, GATT 1994 or TRIPs that would alter the rights and obligations of members will take effect for those members upon acceptance by a two-thirds majority, and thereafter for any member accepting it. There are similar provisions for amendments to Parts I (scope and functions), II (general obligations) and III (specific commitments) of GATS and respective annexes.

The Ministerial Conference could decide that any such amendment to GATT 1994 or TRIPs or GATS, altering rights and obligations, is of such a nature that any Member not accepting it within a specified time period shall be free to withdraw from the WTO or remain a Member with the consent of the Ministerial Conference. But any such decision requires a three-fourths majority of the Members. The analogous provisions in GATT 1947 – Article XXX.2 read with Article XXV.4 – require only a simple majority of votes cast.

Amendments to WTO, GATT 1994 and TRIPs or Parts IV (progressive liberalization), V (institutional provisions) and VI (final provisions) of GATS that do not alter rights and obligations of members will take effect for all members on acceptance by two-thirds of its members.

Unlike GATT 1947 which was only a provisional treaty, the WTO will be a definitive treaty – but not a self-executing one under the US Constitution. Under Article XVI.4 of the WTO, each member 'shall ensure conformity of its laws, regulations and administrative procedures with its obligations provided in the annexed Agreements'.

### *The WTO and Its Dispute Settlement*

For a correct appreciation, the WTO must be read with the DSU. Any dispute among WTO members, arising out of the WTO or its annexed multilateral agreements or the provisions of the DSU itself (under Article 1) is subject to the DSU which, while seemingly procedural and merely codifying and assembling together the current practices, creates some substantive rights and obligations among its members.

Article 23 of the DSU provides that Members seeking redress of violation of obligations or other nullification or impairment of benefits under the covered agreements or an impediment to attainment of any objective of the covered agreements 'shall have recourse to and abide by the rules and procedures' of the DSU. In such cases,

> Members shall
>
> (a) not make a determination to the effect that a violation has occurred, that benefits have been nullified or impaired or that the attainment of any objective of the covered agreements has been impaired, except through recourse to dispute settlement in accordance with the rules and procedures of this Understanding ... .
>
> ....

> (c) follow the procedures set forth in Art. 22 to determine the level of suspension of concessions or other obligations and obtain DSB (Dispute Settlement Body) authorization in accordance with those procedures before suspending concessions or other obligations ... .

This appears to rule out any scope for any unilateral actions (such as under US Trade Act Section 301 laws) and makes any violation a ground for dispute. Any unilateral US trade actions – whether in goods, services or intellectual property rights – would be hit by the provisions of the annexed agreements and the DSU.

At every stage of the dispute settlement process, the DSU has specified for time-limitations, and for automaticity – from the stage of reference of a dispute to a panel to the adoption of its recommendations, and ultimately in authorizing withdrawal of concessions or 'retaliation'. In the present GATT, by long practice, decisions are taken only by consensus and this applies to the adoption of panel rulings and recommendations in the GATT Council. A single country can thus block adoption. Under the WTO-DSU, the inverse is true. A consensus would be needed to *block* reference to a panel and at every subsequent stage, including for setting aside a panel ruling and not adopting the recommendations. There will however be no automatic adoption of recommendations in disputes (never raised so far) that are covered by GATT Article XXIII.1.(c), that is, disputes involving existence of 'any other situation' than failure to carry out an obligation or application of a measure whether or not in conflict with an obligation.

There will be an appeal procedure to an Appellate body on issues of law and legal interpretations by a panel. There are provisions enabling cross-retaliation (withdrawal of concessions in one area for failure to observe obligations in another area), circumscribed though it is by the provision for arbitration on the level of 'suspension' or 'retaliation' and the gradations of actions for cross-retaliation. This will work against the developing countries – and in fact is aimed at them. Any of the industrialized countries, particularly the United States, complaining about violations in the area of TRIPs or services, could easily show (after a panel ruling in their favor) that there could be no meaningful retaliation in these areas and the only area for retaliation is in the goods sector. It has been suggested by some that a complaining developing country, with only essential goods imports coming from a developed party violating its rights, and which would be hurting itself in raising duties on them by way of retaliation, could argue that it could retaliate only via TRIPs or GATS. But this is just theory. In practice it would find it very difficult to do this.

The DSU affirms a preference for implementation of the recommendations, and compensation or retaliation (withdrawal of equivalent concessions) as only a second-best remedy. But if a country against which a ruling is given is unable or refuses to implement, and is not agreeable to compensate the complaining party (by providing some other trade concession), the only remedy for the complaining party is retaliation – the intention being that the retaliatory trade sanctions would persuade the other party to agree to comply.

But this is a remedy that a weaker party will not be able to exercise. And even in the case of a stronger party, it does not really help. If country A is aggrieved by B's restrictions on imports of 'x' from A (often put in place because of domestic producers of 'x' or equivalent products) in violation of B's obligations, and B is asked to remove the restrictions but does not, A can only retaliate against some imports into A from B, say product 'y' coming from B. This may balance the mercantilist books of A, but will not help or compensate the exporter of 'x' in A and will penalize the exporter of 'y' in B for no fault of that exporter either.

However, the current state of international law, in cases of violation, has no enforcement beyond enabling a party to a treaty to denouncing it on grounds of violation by another. Forcing a country to comply with a treaty obligation by going to war would be contrary to the UN Charter.

The only solution, and an effective one, would be for all Contracting Parties to act together, and for each to withdraw some benefit from the party which is refusing or is unable to implement a panel ruling. This has been talked about in the GATT, but has never happened, since in reality the trading system, despite all talk of 'free trade', is a mercantilist one and each Contracting Party wants to benefit from the other's misfortune.

While on paper the WTO system and the DSU make illegal any unilateral interpretations and determination of violation by any one Party to any agreement, what happens in practice will depend on how much any affected Party is willing to stand up and assert its rights; it also presupposes (as all international treaties do) the 'good faith' of its members. But some US statements and assertions of its right, and intention, to continue to use Section 301 laws and other unilateral instruments,[26] cast some doubts on US good faith and *bona fides* in negotiating and accepting the WTO.

The conclusion of the Uruguay Round negotiations with its various agreements including the WTO Agreement, has been hailed as an event of historic importance and one that would create a new trade order in a new world order. The last GATT and the first WTO Director-General Peter Sutherland (July 1993–April 1995) characterized it as a 'defining moment in history'.[27]

## THE WTO AND THE NEW WORLD ORDER

In the weeks before the conclusion of the Uruguay Round, there were a number of econometric projections about the benefits from the Round to the world economy. Welfare gains of US $250 billion after ten years, additional trade gains ranging from $750 billion to several trillion dollars have been bandied about – all on a closer reading are based on a series of variables and assumptions (inflation, exchange rates, monetary and financial policies, etc.), any one or several of which could go wrong. A look at the record of short-term projections, official and non-official, of the last few years should inject a note of caution against over-reliance on projections and predictions. No policymaker and no private investor would take decisions on such projections. At the time these projections were made, even the actual tariff and other concessions had not been finalized; they were settled and the details became known only after Marrakesh.

From the time of Adam Smith and David Ricardo to the present, over a span of more than two centuries, the record of industrial capitalism and *laissez-faire* economics is quite mixed. The collapse of central planning should not blind one to this mixed record. Trade and trade liberalizations do not produce wealth or jobs; they only help in the distribution of demand and jobs. However efficient the 'market' is in allocating resources, the record of three centuries shows that it does not bring about equity and is primarily responsible for the ecological devastation of the planet.

Most of the predictions about the outcome of the Uruguay Round and about the future of the WTO and its trade order are efforts to reassure and lull the public about a future with many uncertainties. Politicians and social scientists, including economists, love 'order'. But 'order' and 'certainty' are not part of nature.[28]

The WTO agreement, coming after the end of the Cold War (with the United States seen as the 'winner' and sole superpower in the US-ordained world order), and at a time of several fiftieth anniversaries (like that of the Bretton Woods, the UN Charter, and the Allied landings in Normandy marking the start of Europe's liberation from Hitler's New Order), has generated a nostalgic view that the post-war vision could be recreated with a new world order – with transnational corporations (TNCs) and a Triad-centered (North America, Europe and Japan) capitalism globalizing the world economy. Developing countries figure very little in these visions.

The institutional framework of the new world order is being envisioned in terms of the trade, monetary and financial systems that are managed and governed by the WTO, IMF and World Bank. Critics of this new world order have described these institutions as the 'Holy Trinity' of the Market God which often behave and attempt to lay down the law, apparently having overtaken or overthrown all other gods and philosophies!

The post-war scheme leading to Bretton Woods was conceived as part of a wider and more comprehensive scheme of international cooperation to cover other topics. In the British discussions, the monetary policy and arrangement were seen as part of other arrangements – including a stabilization policy for cost of living through steps to mitigate fluctuation of international prices of primary commodities, and a trade liberalization policy to remove obstacles to British exports. But Keynes recognized, for example, that without currency agreements (to prevent countries from altering the value of their currencies without agreements and at short notice) there was no firm ground to discuss tariffs:

> Whilst other schemes are not essential as prior proposals to the monetary scheme, it may well be argued, I think, that a monetary scheme gives a firm foundation on which the others can be built. It is very difficult while you have monetary chaos to have order of any kind in other directions ... [I]f we are less successful than we hope for in other directions, monetary proposals instead of being less necessary will be all the more necessary. If there is going to be great difficulty in planning trade owing to tariff obstacles, that makes it all the more important that there should be an agreed orderly procedure for altering exchanges ... [S]o far from monetary proposals depending on the rest of the pro-

> gramme, they should be the more necessary if that programme is less successful than we all hope it is going to be.[29]

The WTO's annexed agreements on trade concessions – with emphasis on price competition and tariff as the main, or only, instrument for import protection and insistence on eliminating any quantitative or other restrictions – are written as if the variation of prices arising out of exchange-rate movements is not of any consequence and that with floating exchange rates the competitive devaluation experience of the inter-war years and its Great Depression are no longer relevant.

The only area where exchange-rate variation is dealt with is in the Agreement on Agriculture which has special safeguard provisions relating to prices of imported agricultural products arising out of such exchange-rate variations.[30] This enables additional import duties, specified at intervals of 10–40 per cent, 40–60 per cent, 60–75 per cent and over 75 per cent of average product prices[31] over the 1986–88 period. Unlike the general 'safeguard' provisions of the GATT, there need be no injury test *vis-a-vis* domestic producers before invocation of safeguards.

The other agreements, including the provisions relating to tariff concessions on non-agricultural products, do not deal with exchange-rate variations. At one stage before the launch of the negotiations, the IMF presented a paper suggesting that short-term exchange-rate fluctuations did not matter *vis-a-vis* trade because traders could hedge their risks in the forward markets. That this was a costly operation for developing countries and their enterprises was ignored or shrugged off. On other occasions, the IMF addresses the adverse effects and difficulties for the developing countries in managing their foreign reserves and external debt. Even then, the IMF does not consider that exchange-rate fluctuations and misalignments result in wrong price signals and affect short, medium and long-term trade and investment decisions and that they generate great pressures in the developed trading partners for protection, particularly against imports of the developing world.[32]

At Punta del Este, the European Community had raised the issue of currency exchange-rate variations and the need to deal with this issue. Everyone understood this was a European counter to the pressure on it over agriculture and an end to the variable levies. There was no consensus on the question and like a number of other issues that were raised – including restrictive business practices, competition policies, debt, trade-labor standards linkage that the United States raised – it was mentioned in the Chairman's concluding statement as one of the issues that could be taken up at the GATT Council. From time to time during the negotiations, particularly when there was pressure on it over agriculture, and also when the exchange rate of the dollar *vis-a-vis* European currencies fell sharply, the European Community reverted to this issue. But no action was ever taken. There is no evidence either that the Executive Directors of the IMF from EC countries ever pursued this seriously in the Fund. The issue was raised at Marrakesh too, and is among the subjects mentioned in the concluding remarks of the Chairman of the Marrakesh Ministerial meeting, Uruguay's Foreign Minister Sergio Abreu Bonilla, who listed all the issues raised by Ministers in their statements and which could be discussed by the WTO Preparatory Committee. The issue is mentioned as 'interaction between trade policies and policies relating to financial and monetary matters, including debt, and commodity markets'.

The world in the 1980s in which the Uruguay Round was launched is very different from that of 1994 when it was concluded.[33] The political map of the world has changed. The Berlin Wall has collapsed and a reunified Germany is becoming once again a dominant power in Europe, particularly Central Europe; the Soviet Union has imploded into its constituent republics but with many question marks about Russia and its relationships with the other former Soviet republics. The system of central planning has been abandoned in the former Soviet Union and East Europe and the 'market' ideology is now supreme.

But, as we move towards the next millennium, the initial euphoria with which these events were greeted – Fukuyama's history has come to an end and George Bush's new world order – has given way to many questions, doubts, caution and uncertainties about the 'New Order'.[34] By mid-1994, the Communist parties had begun making a comeback in elections in Latvia, Poland and Hungary. This does not mean central planning is back, only that people are not ready to swallow *laissez-faire* capitalism and the Fund/Bank fundamentalist ideology of present sacrifices being rewarded in the future.

All, or virtually all developing countries have launched policies of liberalization and have embraced the doctrine of the market. At the same time, the industrialized world which has been preaching these doctrines, but not practicing them, is erecting new barriers against the South on grounds of protecting the environment and social standards; this when the causes of the continuing environmental degradation and falling social standards in the North are to be found within the North, and not in the South.

In 1992, the nations of the world met in Rio de Janeiro at the UN Conference on Environment and Development – the Earth Summit – where they adopted the Rio Declaration, Agenda 21, Programme of Action and other documents, and signed two treaties (on Climate Change and Biological Diversity, which have entered into force). All these together sought to reconcile some conflicts and set the world on a new path, through the concepts of environment and sustainable development.

The overall thrust was that developing countries would need to grow and use more energy and resources to satisfy the needs of their population and to eradicate poverty; the industrial countries would have to change their consumption patterns and wasteful resource use. Since Rio, there has been a steady retreat from the commitments of the heads of state/governments. Rather than set the world on a new path, the patterns of the North are fostered in the South by the liberalization of trade in some 'services' (audio-visual services, western television programs and films, advertising, etc.).

In the industrialized world, and particularly within the United States, the change of administrations has brought a new generation to power, and with it, a changed emphasis and philosophy. President Clinton and his major economic policy advisers clearly favor an interventionist state role in economics, at least at home; bilaterally, they push neo-mercantilist and managed trade policies. These contradictory forces and policies, some beneficial perhaps and many others not so beneficial or reactionary, are still at play and with the final outcome none too certain.

The rules and disciplines laid down in the WTO's annexed agreements go beyond the normal meaning of 'trade', namely goods crossing the frontiers of a country and entering the domestic market. They cover areas of economic activity within countries and within sovereign domestic jurisdictions, that is, production and production processes within a country. As they begin to be implemented, the effects and implications will become more visible inside each country. The resulting clash of interests inside countries and how they will be reconciled are not easy to foretell, despite the optimistic projections of its protagonists and some econometricians. It could be full of surprises and turbulence.

## THE WTO AND OTHER INTERNATIONAL ORGANIZATIONS

The WTO has no explicit provisions about its relationships with the United Nations. In fact, it does not even mention the United Nations. Article V.1 of the WTO merely enables the WTO's General Council to make appropriate arrangements for effective cooperation with other intergovernmental organizations that have responsibilities related to those of the WTO – and thus with the United Nations. But Article 57 of the UN Charter requires every specialized agency to be 'brought into relationship with the United Nations in accordance with the provisions of Article 63 of the Charter'. Since every member of the WTO is also a member of the UN, it therefore has a Charter obligation that overrides any other.

But Article III.5 of the WTO provides that 'with a view to achieving greater coherence in global economic policymaking, the WTO shall cooperate, as appropriate, with the International Monetary Fund and the International Bank for Reconstruction and Development and its affiliated agencies'.

This is buttressed by a separate 'Declaration on the Contribution of the World Trade Organization to Achieving Greater Coherence in Global Economic Policymaking'. The Declaration, which is an integral part of the Final Act, talks of the Uruguay Round agreements and liberal trading policies contributing to healthy growth and development of each country's economy and of the world economy as a whole; of successful cooperation in each area of economic policy contributing to progress in other areas; of greater exchange-rate stability contributing towards expansion of trade; of the need for adequate and timely flow of concessional and non-concessional financial and real investment resources to developing countries and further efforts to address the debt problem; of trade liberalization being an increasingly important component in the success of adjustment programs often involving significant transitional social costs, and of the World Bank and IMF supporting adjustment to trade liberalization including support to net food-importing developing countries.

There is also talk of the positive outcome of the Uruguay Round being a major contribution towards more coherent and complementary international economic policies, and that the improvements to the multilateral trading system would enable trade policy in the future to play a more substantial role in ensuring coherence of global economic policymaking.

There is also the affirmation that interlinkages between the different aspects of economic policy require that the international institutions with responsibilities in each of these areas follow consistent and mutually supportive policies and that the WTO should pursue and develop cooperation with the international institutions responsible for monetary and financial matters, while respecting the mandate, confidentiality requirements and the necessary autonomy in decision making procedures of each institution and 'avoiding' the imposition on governments of cross-conditionality or additional conditions. All these are at best nice sentiments.

The WTO Director-General has been invited to review with the IMF Managing Director and the President of the World Bank, the implications of the WTO's responsibility for its cooperation with the BWIs, as well as forms such cooperation might take, with a view to achieving greater coherence in global economic policymaking. The basic problems of macroeconomic policy and the interdependence of issues and their intergovernmental level of consideration are totally ignored. Who deals with exchange-rate questions and issues of interdependence? For example, if exchange rates are out of line, because of policy misalignments, say amongst the United States, Europe and Japan, and this produces trade deficits in one and surpluses in another, resulting inevitably in trade tensions and even bashing each other in public, who can or will deal with these, more so when these impinge on political decision making? Can the secretariats of the three (World Bank, WTO and IMF), each anxious to preserve their own turf, produce a solution through their consultations? Can the combination of the intergovernmental bodies of the three deal with them or should they be dealt with more appropriately at the UN (ECOSOC or UNCTAD) where the issues can be discussed in an overall framework. If they are not discussed in such a political forum, but dealt with in these IFIs and WTO, can they really be transmitted into national policies in a coordinated way?

In effect the WTO is trying to achieve what Keynes and others saw was not possible, namely trade liberalization and tariff reductions and bindings in a non-functioning monetary and financial system. In the floating exchange-rate monetary system presided over by the Fund, currency rates are being driven up or down, not by underlying economic factors or actions of a government, but by speculative movements of short-term capital which is totally distorting price signals for trade, production and investment. The financial system is such that there is no intermediation by the Bank to ensure global mobilization of savings and capital to be put to productive use for satisfying people's needs. The Bank's annual net transfer of capital to the developing world is about $4 billion, compared to the gross fixed capital formation in the entire developing world of an annual $300 billion[35] or about one per cent.

The WTO theoretically has one-state one-vote and consensus decision making. The IMF and World Bank have a one-dollar one-vote basis for their governance and are run by their managements for the benefit of the major shareholders and in the interests of their transnational corporations (TNCs). There are fears that the combination of the World Bank, the WTO and the IMF will be undemocratic and the trio thus will try to control the South and former East in the interests of the North and its TNCs.

The Uruguay Round, unlike the earlier GATT rounds, was really all about restructuring the international economic system, rolling back the state and opening up the Third World for the transnationalization of their economies. It was always presented officially as bringing under multilateral rules and disciplines sectors of trade and important areas of economic activity – agriculture, textiles and clothing and services – outside international disciplines and to liberalize the trade in these US sectors and enable trade-offs among these. In some areas, such as in TRIPs, a high moralistic tone was adopted in order to present US/EC demands as a measure to prevent some kind of 'criminal activity' – piracy, theft and counterfeiting – rather than its reality, namely, to ensure *rentier* incomes for the TNCs through global monopoly rights – the antithesis of liberalization.

But by 1990, some of the WTO's protagonists began to talk about the real nature of the Uruguay Round negotiations, that is, to create level playing fields for TNCs and for the transnationalization of production, trade, distribution and consumption of goods and services.[36] The final outcome has perhaps created such level playing fields for the TNCs; at the same time, it has created many hills and moats in the path of peoples in all countries and for their domestic enterprises.

The new WTO trade order will foreclose for developing countries several of the development options that today's industrialized countries pursued to accumulate capital and knowledge and reach their present affluence. And while the developing countries remain nominally independent, the State will not protect the people, but treat unequals as equals and protect the foreign capital and the TNCs. The combined effect of the policies and ideologies of the BWIs and the WTO's new trade order will be to push the developing world back, in economic terms, to the colonial era when the State was run for the benefit of the metropolitan capital and to perpetuate that unjust and iniquitous international division of labor which the peoples of the South had hoped they could overcome. Developing countries are now told that their post-independence quest for economic autonomy is 'unattainable' and that the 'world stands on the threshold of a new era which, while in some respects is a harkback to the golden years of the nineteenth century, is likely to be qualitatively different'. Developing countries have to accept and embrace the emerging 'alliance capitalism'[37] – a neocolonial regionalization under the Triad.

If this happens, and the predictions and projections of prosperity for all (through the trickle-down effects) do not materialize, it may prove to be a prescription for social disorders. Revolutionary changes in technology and communications have enabled the 'globalization' phenomenon, but have also brought to the poor in the South daily images of how the rich North and the rich in the South live. Such visible disparities and conspicuous consumption flaunted before the poor are not a foundation for peace and stability. Any order built on these premises is built on foundations of sand.

A stable order would need some fundamental changes to the monetary and finance systems and their governance in order to ensure monetary and exchange-rate stability, control of private speculative capital and a world not biased towards deflation. Instead, a stable order would promote employment – and a trade system that provides space for the developing countries, rather than closes their development options as the new WTO now would do, and brings some control and discipline on the TNCs.

Within the trade system, the WTO and its annexed agreements would need modifications to restore to each national government, the power and responsibility to judge the roles and limitations of the market and its regulation with the public interest in mind. The WTO has also to accept the reality of the rich–poor gap in the world, and the problems facing the late entrants; it must provide contractually enforceable special privileges (and not special disabilities as under the Multi-Fibre Arrangement) to the developing world, corresponding to their state of development.

Within countries, and certainly in the advanced industrialized states, the political economy of the country and the policies to be pursued are subject to democratic governance and determined after public debate by political processes. At the international level, and particularly with reference to the Fund and the Bank, this fundamental has to be brought home. Under the guise of 'technical' and 'financial' institutions, they should not be allowed to usurp the function of policy definitions and their limitations and decisions, and the integration of global economic and social policies for sustainable development (understood in its real sense, that is, curing the maldevelopment of the over-developed North and the development of the under-developed South in the interests of all peoples). These are essentially political functions that ought to be in the domain of international political economy and hence in the United Nations and ECOSOC. Only such an architecture can help the world move towards a peaceful twenty-first century and on the path of sustainable development for all.

## SUMMARY

The Uruguay Round of multilateral trade negotiations has been concluded with a package of agreements, all of which have been annexed to an agreement to establish the WTO, with every country required to accept all the agreements as a package. It has been hailed as an important achievement and harbinger of a rule-based trading system. Whether the WTO and the new trade order will in fact be a rule-based system depends on how the major industrialized nations behave, and whether they give up their unilateralist and neo-mercantilist approaches. The overall result of the WTO is one of foreclosing to developing countries the options and strategies followed in the past by the present developed countries to reach their present positions, including Japan, and the newly industrialized countries in the post-war period. It thus perpetuates an already asymmetric international trading system.

The WTO has also been hailed as establishing the new trade order in a new world order and completing the architecture contemplated at Bretton Woods: the IMF and the World Bank working in tandem with an International Trade Organization to promote the Bretton Woods objectives of rising standards of living and full employment. However, the Fund and the Bank now have no role or effective power over the industrialized countries. Rather, they act as their instruments to ensure implementation by the developing world and the transition economies of the former socialist bloc of the policies decided by the North and the general ideological approach of furthering the interests of the TNCs. As a result, the trinity of the Fund-Bank-WTO will merely make the international economic system even more asymmetric and oppressive of the poor.

Fundamental changes must be applied to the monetary and financial systems and their governance in order to ensure monetary and exchange-rate stability, control of private speculative capital and a world not biased towards deflation, but promoting employment. A trade system must be implemented that provides space for the developing countries, rather than closes their development options as the new WTO now would do, and that brings some control and discipline on the TNCs. Without these changes, the new trade and economic order will not be a stable one, but rather will create social disorders.

## NOTES

1. Percy Mistry, *Multilateral Debt: An Emerging Crisis?* (The Hague: Forum on Debt and Development (FONDAD), 1994) p. 67.
2. United Nations Conference on Trade and Development (UNCTAD), 'Chapter II: Adjustment and Stagnation in Sub-Saharan Africa', *Trade and Development Report 1993* (New York: United Nations, 1993) pp. 93–111; Manuel Agosin and Diana Tussie (eds), *Trade and Growth: New Dilemmas in Trade Policy* (London: Macmillan, 1993); United Nations Conference on Trade and Development (UNCTAD), *International Monetary and Financial Issues for the 1990s: Research Papers for the Group of Twenty-Four*, Vols I to VI (New York: United Nations, 1993); David Greenaway, 'Liberalizing Foreign Trade Through Rose-Tinted Glasses', *Economic Journal*, vol. 103, no. 416 (January 1993) pp. 208–22; Michel Chossudovsky, 'The "Third Worldisation" of Russia Under IMF Rule', *Third World Economics*, no. 67 (1993) pp. 14–16; Charles Abugre, 'Critique of World Bank/IMF Insistence on More Structural Adjustment Policies for Least Developed Countries', *Third World Economics*, no. 74 (1993) pp. 17–20.
3. This issue figured at the Group of Twenty-Four (G-24) sponsored technical conference in Cartagena in a summary of suggestions:

   > Technical exchanges, unmediated by the IFIs, such as the Cartagena conference, are extremely useful and important. Research papers that are prepared from outside the IFI system are also extremely important to counter its near 'monopoly' of research on the economic problems of developing countries.

See Gerald K. Helleiner, 'Introduction' in United Nations Conference on Trade and Development (UNCTAD), *The International Monetary and Financial System: Developing Country Perspectives* (Geneva: UNCTAD, 1994) p. 20.

4. General Agreement on Tariffs and Trade (GATT), *Trends in International Trade: A Report by a Panel of Experts* (Geneva: GATT, 1958).
5. Named after the beach resort in Uruguay, where the initial meetings were held.
6. Chakravarthi Raghavan, 'The MTO: Promoter of World Trade or New Instrument of Oppression', *Third World Economics*, no. 56–7 (January 1993) pp. 2–17.
7. Chakravarthi Raghavan, *Recolonization: GATT, the Uruguay Round and the Third World* (London and Atlantic Highlands, NJ: Zed Books; and Penang, Malaysia: Third World Network, 1990) pp. 222–4 and 249–51; see also Raghavan, 'The MTO: Promoter of World Trade or New Instrument of Oppression'.
8. Raghavan, *Recolonization: GATT, the Uruguay Round and the Third World*, pp. 1–225.
9. When the General Agreement was put into force, provisionally, from January 1, 1948, by the Protocol of Provisional Application, it was an executive agreement without needing legislative approval or changes. It was to have been a temporary arrangement, pending ratification and entry into force of the Havana Charter. The governments of the signatories to the protocol committed themselves to apply provisionally: (a) Parts I and III of the General Agreement; and (b) Part II of that Agreement 'to the fullest extent not inconsistent with existing legislation'.
10. Section 301 of the 1974 US Trade Act, see Glossary for details.
11. See the *South-North Development Monitor SUNS*, no. 2351 (April 4, 1990): when the European Community presented a draft text for an agreement on Trade-Related Intellectual Property Rights (TRIPs) and was asked how GATT could be used to amend World Intellectual Property Organization (WIPO) conventions, the EC negotiator Peter Morgans Carl told journalists 'anything is possible between consenting adults' in GATT. The agreement on TRIPs effectively amends the Paris Union Conventions and imposes obligations on countries that are not Parties to that Convention.
12. See the *South-North Development Monitor SUNS*, no. 2336 (March 14, 1990) under the headline, 'Group of 77: Negative to Institutionalizing GATT as the ITO'.
13. See the *South-North Development Monitor SUNS*, no. 2405 (June 25, 1990) under the headline, 'Trade: EC proposes an MTO to enlarge and restructure GATT'.
14. Raghavan, 'The MTO: Promoter of World Trade or New Instrument of Oppression'.
15. It is ironic that the World Trade Organization, which is supposed to enhance observance of global norms on intellectual property rights,

(mis)appropriated the acronym WTO which was already registered property of the World Tourism Organization at the World Intellectual Property Organization (WIPO).

16. The agreements concluded at Marrakesh though are incomplete in many areas and the Final Act, through various Ministerial decisions, in fact provides for their continuance – for example in financial services, in basic telecommunications services and in maritime services as well as in regard to movement of natural persons which is one of the four modes for delivery of services. There are also scattered throughout the texts other areas of built-in work programs and negotiations.
17. See speech of Peter Sutherland, GATT Director-General at World Economic Forum, Davos, Switzerland (February 1994) in *GATT Focus Newsletter*, no. 105, p. 6: 'The Uruguay Round may well be the last of its kind, but this in no way means the end of Multilateral Trade Negotiations. On the contrary it means they become permanent.'
18. The WTO was established on January 1, 1995 as 76 countries out of the 128 GATT members had accepted the Uruguay Round agreements and submitted their commitments on trade in goods and services.
19. Original WTO members would be members of the GATT 1947, whose schedules of goods market access and commitments in agriculture and services, have been verified, accepted and annexed.
20. Raghavan, *Recolonization: GATT, the Uruguay Round and the Third World*, pp. 278–9; for the text of the April 1989 Mid-term Accords see GATT document MTN.TNC/11.
21. See Part I.B.(ii) of the Declaration.
22. Ambassador Srirang P. Shukla had forged the two-track compromise with the United States and the European Community at Punta del Este in February 1988.
23. Ambassador Tran Van-Thinh said at a meeting of the Uruguay Round Group of Negotiations on Goods (GNG) on February 18, 1988, that 'globality' for the European Community meant progress and agreements on issues in the Group of Negotiations on Goods (GNG) and in the Group of Negotiations on Services (GNS). Indian Ambassador S.P. Shukla responded that the globality of the Uruguay Round involved only four elements:
    - unity of time and place for the Punta del Este meeting;
    - establishment of a Trade Negotiations Committee (to oversee both the GNG and GNS which respectively were running the goods and services negotiations);
    - common point of time for commencement and conclusion of the two distinct processes of negotiations, and
    - the provision that the decision on the implementation of the results of negotiations in two processes would be taken at a Ministerial meeting on the pattern of that at Punta del Este (a GATT Ministerial Contracting Parties' meeting and a separate meeting of Trade Ministers for Services).

    Shukla continued that 'No other linkage – legal, procedural or otherwise – has been envisaged in the two separate processes of negotiations in goods and services.' See the *South-North Development Monitor SUNS*, no. 1991 (February 20, 1988) pp. 6–7.

24. See Chakravarthi Raghavan, 'The MTO: Promoter of World Trade or New Instrument of Oppression', pp. 2–17.
25. Raghavan, 'The MTO: Promoter of World Trade or New Instrument of Oppression'.
26. See the *South-North Development Monitor SUNS*, no. 3292 (May 6, 1994): 'US to retain Section 301 laws and use them too' (report on letter of US Trade Representative Mickey Kantor to Senator Jesse Helms); Laura D'Andrea Tyson (Chairperson of the US President's Council of Economic Advisers) 'US Triumphant in Trade Policy', *Wall Street Journal*, May 30, 1994.
27. Speech of GATT Director-General Peter Sutherland at Trade Negotiations Commission meeting of December 15, 1993, closing the negotiations; see Peter Sutherland, 'Success', *GATT Focus Newsletter*, no. 104 (1993) pp. 1–4.
28. The uncertainty and random principles of quantum mechanics underlie all of modern science and technology. The entropy (measure of disorder) of the second law of thermodynamics teaches us that disorder or entropy of an isolated system will tend to increase when things are left to themselves and that when two closed systems are joined together, the entropy of the combined system will be more than the sum of the entropies of the individual systems. And cosmology has moved from its original inflationary model at the beginning to the chaotic inflationary model. See Stephen W. Hawking, *A Brief History of Time: From the Big Bang to Black Holes* (Toronto and New York: Bantam Books, 1988) pp. 54–6, p. 102 and pp. 127–32.
29. John Maynard Keynes, 'Letter to Lord Addison of May 1944' in John M. Keynes, *The Collected Writings of John Maynard Keynes* (Cambridge: Macmillan and Cambridge University Press, 1980) Vol. XXVI pp. 5–6.
30. Article 5 of the Agreement on Agriculture.
31. The average prices are expressed in domestic currency and including costs for insurance and freight (cif).
32. United Nations Conference on Trade and Development (UNCTAD), *The Exchange Rate System, International Monetary and Financial Issues for Developing Countries* (Geneva: UNCTAD, 1987) pp. 77–123; for the effects on trade and production of developing countries see pp. 86–8.
33. Raghavan, *Recolonization: GATT, the Uruguay Round and the Third World*, pp. 32–78.
34. Chakravarthi Raghavan, 'The New World Order and North-South Relations', *Resurgence*, no. 9 (May 1991) p. 16; and Andre Gunder Frank, Johan Galtung, Immanuel Wallerstein and Chakravarthi Raghavan, 'Overview of the Global Scene' in Kaarle Nordenstreng and Herbert Schiller (eds) *Beyond National Sovereignty* (New Jersey: Ablex, 1993) pp. 3–81.

35. UNCTAD computations from the IMF's *International Financial Statistics* data bank.
36. Sylvia Ostrey, 'Help the Three Systems Sing in Harmony', *International Herald Tribune*, April 19, 1990.
37. John H. Dunning, *Globalization, Economic Restructuring and Development: The Prebisch Lecture for 1994* (Geneva: UNCTAD, 1994).

# 2 The Social Dimensions of Economic Integration

*Stephen R. Sleigh*

## INTRODUCTION

The North American Free Trade Agreement (NAFTA) signed by President Bush in December 1992, pushed ardently by President Clinton and approved by the US House of Representatives and Senate in November 1993, presented an opportunity to shape and formalize the process of regional economic integration (between the United States, Mexico and Canada), that has occurred during recent years in an unregulated manner. Narrowing the focus of these talks to the elimination of trade barriers and the reduction of tariffs provided policymakers with a well-known formula for increasing trade. To the extent that this time-tested General Agreement on Tariffs and Trade (GATT) formula actually leads toward greater economic efficiency and breaks down distorting or protectionist trade policy in the region, mainstream economic theory predicts so much the better for everyone in the long run. Besides numerous technical problems with NAFTA, there are legitimate concerns about the way in which the predicted gains from freer trade are distributed. The important question, which was not a formal part of the NAFTA or GATT negotiations, is who will benefit and who will lose from increasing economic integration. There is a social or distributional dimension to the NAFTA and other trade-related agreements that policymakers must address in a coherent fashion, rather than as an afterthought, in order to insure that the benefits of trade agreements are distributed fairly.

The aim of this chapter is to develop a framework for the development of a multilateral effort that has the support of business, labor and government that would provide a mechanism for dealing with the social dimensions of economic integration, specifically those dealing with labor market issues. Important concerns over the environmental impact of trade agreements pose further concerns worthy of detailed debate. The first section of this chapter reviews current data on the likely impact of NAFTA on employment levels. The data is presented with considerable qualification. The general equilibrium models used to project economic trends can, at best, serve as guideposts for predicting the future direction of a dynamic economy. Despite the serious limitations of these predictions, an emerging consensus indicates that the short-term adjustment problems for some industries, let alone specific enterprises, will be severe. Coming at a time of recent economic recovery from recessions in the United States and Canada, the negative aspects of NAFTA will disrupt employment in many industries in the United States, Canada and Mexico. The European Community faced similar questions when economic integration was proposed for a European Common Market. The comparison between NAFTA and the European Common Market is more than just a passing academic interest.

Following this introduction, the next section gives an overview of the economic impact of further North American economic integration. Then, the example of the European Community's response to the social dimensions of integration will be analyzed. The European Social Charter, which emerged in 1988 out of intense negotiations between European business, labor and government, addresses many of the concerns that labor organizations have raised in North America about NAFTA. The Social Charter for the European Common Market has generally failed to live up to the hopes of European labor organizations, or the fears of European business. The negotiations over the European Social Charter present a vivid example of the difficulties of building consensus among business, labor and government on cross-national trade-related issues. In sharp contrast to Europe, labor organizations are generally weaker in North America, making it even less likely that a full-blown social charter will find sufficient support or acceptance to become institutionalized in North America.

The final section proposes a different approach to dealing with the social dimensions of North American integration than the adoption of a North American social charter. The idea hinges on the relationship between the universality of worker rights along with vigorous enforcement of these rights and economic growth. Worker rights provide the common thread that binds together a universal approach to the social dimensions of economic integration. The approach is one that would permit economies to structurally adjust to the greatest extent possible without erecting efficiency-distorting barriers while allowing, and even encouraging, workers an equal place in the process through bargaining with employers over the terms and conditions of work with employers. The International Labor Organisation (ILO), together with international trade and finance organizations such as the World Bank, GATT, and the International Monetary Fund (IMF), could provide the basis for this new approach to the social dimensions of economic integration. The obstacles to creating viable mechanisms that would enforce worker rights across national borders are many. A social pact between business, labor and government in North America that commits the social partners to develop and support the principles behind such an idea could provide a meaningful starting point.

## EMPLOYMENT AND DISTRIBUTIONAL EFFECTS OF NAFTA

Since President Bush notified the US Congress on September 25, 1990 that the United States and Mexico intended to initiate negotiations for a free trade agreement, debate has swirled over consequences of such an agreement on jobs, workers and their communities in both the United States and Mexico. From the outset, organized labor in the United States has raised doubts about the positive impacts of the free trade agreement with as strong a voice as it could muster. For months the unions of the American Federation of Labor and Congress of Industrial Organizations (AFL-CIO), along with a wide array of other groups, lobbied senators and congressional representatives to deny the President the ability to negotiate a trade agreement under the fast-track procedures of the 1988 Omnibus Trade Bill. Despite a concerted effort, which included concern over human rights abuses, the environmental effects of the *maquiladoras* (in-bond manufacturing industry), migration patterns, government protection of agriculture and drug trafficking in Mexico, the fast-track provision was extended in a vote of 231–192 in May 1991. Armed with congressional approval, President Bush and his chief trade negotiator Carla Hills, set to work to bring about a comprehensive North American Free Trade Agreement.

Predicting the impact of NAFTA on jobs in the United States, Mexico and Canada is clearly an inexact science. Before looking at some of the studies that indicate the magnitude of job loss and job creation to be expected due to NAFTA, a few points must be made.

First, the opening of economic relations between the United

States and Mexico is the continuation of a process begun several years ago and codified in three recent accords: the Understanding and Framework for Trade and Investment (1987), a similar Understanding to Facilitate Trade and Investments (1989) and the Understanding to Set Up a Joint Committee for Promotion of Investment and Trade (1989). These three agreements not only provided forums in which discussion to decrease trade barriers took place, but also provided a formal structure to promote business opportunities in both the United States and Mexico.[1] The groundwork for opening the Mexican economy to foreign investment, initiated in earlier Mexican regimes but taken to new levels by the Mexican President Carlos Salinas de Gotari in a process some have called 'Salinas-troika', provides an indication of the scale, scope and impact increased foreign investment is likely to have on jobs in the United States and Mexico.

Second, the signing of a free trade agreement with Canada in 1988, that served in many ways as a model for US–Mexican negotiations, provides an indication of the transferability of jobs. Given the relative parity in wages and overall labor costs between the United States and Canada, the comparison to Mexico is of limited value. However, one would expect that the magnitude and direction of the impact would be clear. The actual magnitude and direction of job loss in Canada in fact has bolstered the arguments of opponents of NAFTA in the United States. Over the last three years 315,000 jobs, mostly in manufacturing, were relocated from Canada to areas with less restrictive regulations and lower labor costs, including the United States.[2] In Canada the political consequences of the free trade agreement resonated in the anti-free trade direction.

Third, and most important from the perspective of the social dimensions of NAFTA, are the distributional aspects of trade liberalization. Even if the logic and economics of comparative advantage were undisputed and uni-directional in a win-win scenario for all countries, there would remain the question of the distribution of gains. The United States, for example, grew economically through most of the 1980s, providing nearly 17 million new jobs. The expansion, which came to an abrupt halt in July 1990, resulted in a far greater number of jobs, but also in an increasingly unequal distribution of wealth. The lesson from the 1980s is that economic growth that is concentrated at the top trickles down far too slowly to ameliorate social ills. If the push for increasing trade liberalization is to gain widespread support it must include a social dimension that will ensure an equitable distribution of gains.

Finally, there are political concerns in the United States and Mexico that evolve from the long history between the two countries. The opening up of the Mexican economy, beginning in 1990 under President Salinas has not always translated into an opening or democratizing of Mexican politics. There is a lively debate, fueled by the mixed experiences of countries in Eastern Europe and the Soviet Union, whether economic liberalization must precede political democratization. In the context of US-Mexican relations the historical reluctance of Mexico to follow political directions from Washington can be expected to continue in the future. The challenge will remain to find an effective way to couple economic growth and trade liberalization with political openness and democratic participation. The policy approach in this chapter focuses on the possibilities of removing these problems from a bilateral or regional basis by putting them into a more universal, multilateral framework. This approach is developed below.

Data on the likely impact of NAFTA are, as noted above, subject to qualification. In September 1990 the US House Committee on Ways and Means and the Senate Committee on Finance requested that the International Trade Commission (ITC) conduct an investigation of the likely economic impact on the United States of a free trade agreement with Mexico. The report was completed in February 1991. The conclusion of the report was that a free trade agreement with Mexico would expand trade opportunities, lower prices, increase competition and result in savings from a larger scale of production. Because the gains from liberalizing trade with Mexico would outweigh the costs, the ITC study concluded that the US economy would on balance benefit from a free trade agreement over the long run.[3]

The ITC analysis cautiously noted that the relative size of the economies of the United States, Canada and Mexico alone mitigates against large structural imbalances in the United States. With a gross domestic product (GDP) of $5,167 billion in 1989, the US economy is nearly ten times larger than Canada's ($543 billion) and 28 times larger than Mexico's ($187 billion). In relative terms, the expansion that may result from NAFTA will have limited overall effect on the US economy. The greatest impact, it would seem, is in the prospect of a rapidly expanding Mexican economy. The combined economic power of a North American trading bloc, with total output close to $6 trillion and 364 million consumers would make it 25 per cent larger than the European Community.

The difficulty with the ITC study, and others done with traditional economic models in mind, is that NAFTA represents a trade agreement without historical precedent: a low-wage, developing country opening its borders to trade with a large, developed country. It is worth noting that the economic disparity between northern and southern European countries is far less than between the United States and Mexico. The GDP per capita in Germany, the wealthiest country in the European Community (EC) in terms of overall economic production and per capita income, is 3.5 times larger than in Greece, and 4.5 times larger than Portugal, the poorest EC nation in per capita income. In comparison, the per capita GDP in the United States is 11 times larger than in Mexico.[4] Alternative estimates are not so optimistic about the positive results of NAFTA for employment levels in the United States. Before the peso collapse of 1994, it was predicted that capital flows were likely to increase dramatically to Mexico on a sustainable basis, especially if the banking reform becomes a reality, both in the United States and Mexico, that would make transferring capital easier. One study estimated that US direct investment in Mexico is likely to rise between $4.35 billion and $5.9 billion in the first years of NAFTA. The estimated cumulative additional investment flow from the United States to Mexico would amount to between $31.2 billion and $52.7 billion by the year 2000. The overall effect on US jobs of this shifting of direct investment capital is the estimated loss of between 260,000 and 439,000 jobs over the same time period.[5]

Clearly the difference to the US economy between moderate growth due to liberalized trade and the opening of markets in Mexico, and the loss of thousands of jobs due to the transfer of direct investments from the US to Mexico, is at the heart of the problem with NAFTA. With such a huge disparity in wages and other social costs, including environmental regulation, the incentive is great for US producers to move into low-wage Mexican operations. The Bureau of Labor Statistics data for 1990 showed that for all manufacturing production workers across industries, compensation costs in Mexico were $1.85 per hour, or 12 per cent the US level of $14.83 – a figure that has fallen from 34 per cent in 1981 despite the liberalization of Mexican trade relations.[6] Without adequate social institutions or regulation, the incentive to exploit this labor-cost differential will result in a vicious cycle of mobile capital moving in and out of speculative investments leaving behind more working poor in both countries.

The evidence for this is striking in the United States. During the last 15 years – the era of government deregulation that began with President Carter and expanded dramatically in subsequent Republican administrations, the gulf between rich and poor in the United States has grown markedly. Despite the fact that the overall economy grew during the 1980s, adding jobs while most developed countries were stagnant, the median wage declined. In manufacturing, compensation declined in real terms from 1979 to 1988 while annual increases were achieved in West Germany (2.4 per cent annual growth rate), Japan (2.1 per cent), and Canada (1 per cent).[7] The decline in manufacturing jobs and wages went together with rising income inequality throughout the US economy as a whole. Figures for 1990 show that the share of total income that went to households in the highest 20 per cent income bracket rose from 43.3 per cent in 1970 to 44.1 per cent in 1980 to 46.6 per cent in 1990.[8] The concentration of wealth in the highest 1 per cent of Americans has grown the most during the last 15 years. Almost all growth in real incomes from 1977 to 1991 has occurred in the top 5 per cent income bracket. While income has remained flat or declined for most during this period, the richest 1 per cent of Americans saw their after-tax income rise by 120 per cent.[9]

The point is clear: an economy can continue to grow, provide more jobs, and at the same time become increasingly unfair, with less equitable distribution of the outcomes of economic growth. For this to occur otherwise, solid social institutions or regulations are needed. A recent study comparing poverty in the United States and Canada came up with solid evidence of this.[10] Using extensive data from 1986 the study found that market forces alone left 17.5 per cent of Canadians poor. Once welfare assistance and other governmental programs were counted, the rate fell to 11.8 per cent. By contrast, the United States started out with less poverty but wound up with more: market forces produced a poverty rate of 15.5 per cent, but government assistance cut that figure only to 13.6 per cent.[11]

Similarly, the decline of trade unions in the United States has broken down an important mechanism for the private determination of income distribution. Particularly marked in the private sector, the decline of unionism in the United States has lessened the ability of workers to negotiate collectively for a larger slice of the economic pie. From 1970 to 1993 union representation of the private sector work-force declined significantly, shown graphically below in Figure 2.1. The figure should not, however, give the impression that organized labor's power or will to fight for the interests of their members has diminished beyond the point of relevance. Despite the serious decline in union density, organized labor remains a potent force in American economic and social life.

For the United States the evidence indicates that the fall in union density contributed to the increasing income inequality in the 1980s. One study based on cross-section-based estimates of the union wage effect suggests that roughly 40 per cent of the rise in the white-collar wage premium and about 16–18 per cent of the rise in the college premium are attributable to the fall in union density.[12]

The reduction of social welfare spending, coupled with the decline of the voluntary system of collective bargaining, has left the United States with a weak system of social provision. In Europe, with much stronger social institutions and trade unions than in North America, a social compact has evolved from the discussions

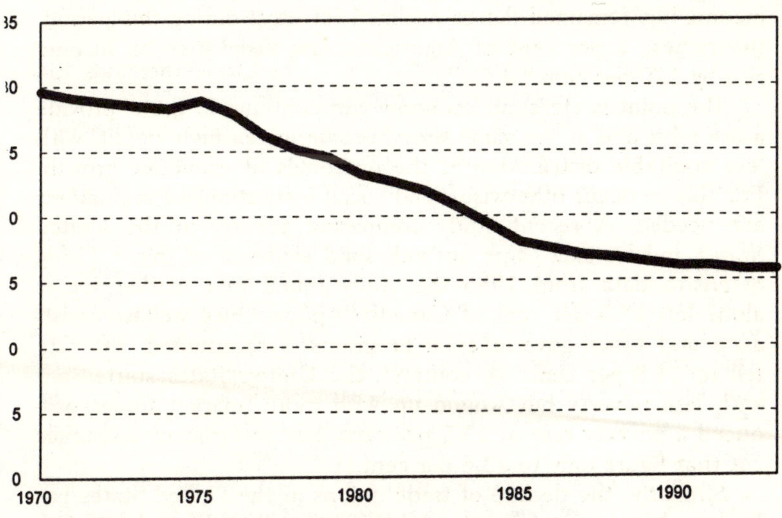


Figure 2.1: Decline in Union Density in the United States (as a percentage of employment).

Source: 1970–84; Henry S. Farber, (1987) 'The Recent Decline of Unionization in the United States', *Science*, vol. 238, no. 4829 (November 13, 1987) p. 915; 1985–93: *US Bureau of Labor Statistics*, various January editions.

about the economic integration of 1992. The Social Charter that has resulted from ongoing negotiations between business, labor and government in Europe is by no means a perfect solution to the problems of the social effects of economic integration. It does however present an example of what could be done in conjunction with regional trade agreements, including NAFTA. The weakness of social institutions in the United States, Canada and Mexico mitigates any realistic chance that trade unions, consumer groups, environmentalists, or others will be able to bring business and government to the bargaining table around a North American social clause. The active presence of multilateral organizations, such as the IMF, World Bank, GATT, or ILO may well provide the needed forum for discussing these issues. Before developing this idea a brief review of the European Social Charter will help put it into perspective.

## SOCIAL DIMENSIONS OF EUROPEAN ECONOMIC INTEGRATION

In 1957, Belgium, France, Italy, Luxemburg, the Netherlands and Germany resolved to form a European Community (EC) in an effort to merge the existing political, social and economic machinery of western Europe. By the turn of the decade in 1980, however, European officials realized that in order to successfully integrate Europe politically, an economic merger would be a necessary prerequisite. Out of this realization the European Economic Community was established with a deadline of the end of 1992 for an economic merger. To make the economic unification a success, European policymakers saw the need for a social reconstruction which would embody a unified European social system. This 'social dimension' of Europe, recognized as early as 1965, has become one of the cornerstones in efforts to achieve economic and political integration.

As stated in the Treaty of Rome in 1957 the main objective of the EC was to achieve four fundamental freedoms: the free and unhindered movement of goods, capital, services and people. The Community acutely observed that the achievements of these freedoms without any type of economic or social unity would become futile. In response to these concerns the European Social Fund was created in the 1960s, with the special objective of eliminating the large socioeconomic disparity between EC member states, which by the early 1980s had grown to twelve.

An objective of the European Social Fund was to establish an effective program in order to create a unified social standard among all its member states. This program was to delineate the minimum labor, health and social requirements of each nation in order to conform with EC standards. By 1974 a Commission was appointed by the European Social Fund which drew up a Social Action Program that laid out the first tangible goals for unified EC social standards.[13] The Social Action Program stated three main objectives for true social unity: full and better employment across Europe, improved living and working conditions, and increasing involvement of labor and industry in EC decisions.

Six specific policies were recommended by the Social Action Program to ensure adequate social integration:

- appropriate consultation between member states on their employment policies, guided by the need to achieve a policy of full and better employment in the Community as a whole;

- a common policy on vocational training, especially an alignment of training standards;

- appropriate coordination of social protection policies of the member states with particular aim of bringing them together;

- a progressive introduction of machinery for adapting social security benefits to increase prosperity in various member states;

- the assistance of trade unions to take part in the Community work to establish training and information services for European affairs, and to create a European Trade Union Institute, and

- the facilitation of conclusive agreements at a European level on appropriate technical and labor matters.

Due to the global depression brought on by the breaking up of the Bretton Woods fixed exchange-rate system and the oil embargo in the early 1970s, the social reconstruction efforts of European integration only received minimal attention, and the Social Action Program was never fully ratified or acted upon. Nevertheless, the recommendations in the Social Action Program proved an invaluable basis for future efforts in European social unification.

Connected to the discussion about the establishment of a European single market in 1992, the issue of social integration was taken up again. Jacques Delors of France proposed a document which was adopted by the European Council in 1989, the Community Charter of the Fundamental Rights of Workers, also known as the European Social Charter. The European Social Charter envisaged an alternate approach to social reconstruction compared to the Social Action Program in that it merely stated ideals and principles, leaving technical aspects of social integration to specialized committees. Working closely with experts from the ILO, the drafters of the European Social Charter came up with a list of principles that closely resemble the conventions of the ILO. The main principles delineated in the charter are:

- the right to freedom of movement,
- the right to employment and minimum remuneration,
- the right to improved living and working conditions,
- the right to social protection,
- the right to freedom of association and collective bargaining,
- the right to vocational training, and
- the right to worker information, consultation, and participation in enterprise decision making.

Although the earlier Charter was drawn up in the 1960s, the EC was unable to get the required unanimous vote for its implementation. When the debate on the Social Charter of 1992 resurfaced in the European Council of Ministers in mid-1989, it still failed to receive a unanimous vote, though only the United Kingdom voted against it. With the full support of the President of the European Commission, Jacques Delors, and widespread support from European trade unionists, the Social Charter idea will not go away. As Mr Delors has said:

> The social dimension permeates all our discussions and everything we do: our efforts to restore competitiveness and co-operate on macroeconomic policy to reduce unemployment and provide all young Europeans with a working future; common

> policies designed to promote the development of less prosperous regions and the regeneration of regions hit by industrial change.[14]

The diversity of industrial relations systems across Europe, from the co-determination policies of Germany to the decentralized craft system in the United Kingdom, disparities in wealth between the northern and southern European countries, and widely divergent levels of trade union strength, all suggest that achieving harmonization on the social and economic plane will prove elusive. Some have argued further that the mechanisms in the Social Charter will protect those in labor and industry who are well organized against the interests of entrepreneurs and workers who fall outside of the scope of collective bargaining. The Social Charter may as a consequence retard employment growth.[15] From another perspective the failure of the European trade union movement to achieve bargaining standards across boundaries is an indication of how far the labor movement's power has declined in Europe since the time of the Social Action Programme.[16]

These criticisms of the European Social Charter certainly deserve fuller analysis than space permits here. The key point is that the notion of the social dimensions of economic integration has received a level of prominence that was distinctly missing in the NAFTA negotiations. A second related point is the recognition that, even given the high level of importance that leading European politicians and relatively powerful trade unions have placed on the social dimensions, building consensus among business, labor and government takes time and concerted effort. By separating labor and environmental issues from the 'real' economic action, the administrations in Ottawa, Washington and Mexico City undermined the chances that a free trade agreement would achieve the inseparable goals of economic growth and fair distribution of gains.

The European Social Charter, despite the limitations noted above, goes a long way towards addressing the fairness and distributional dimensions of European economic integration. Despite the attractiveness of the European Social Charter, it is doubtful that such an approach would work in the North American context due to the generally weak systems of social welfare and the limited ability of labor to bring business to bargain over larger social issues. Another approach is needed, one that recognizes the limits of North American social institutions, the power and mobility of North American capital, the history of cooperation and conflict between the United States, Canada and Mexico, and the commitment by the social partners from business, labor and government to an open world economic trading system. An alternative approach to the social dimensions of North American economic integration that addresses these concerns is sketched below.

## A MULTILATERAL APPROACH TO THE SOCIAL DIMENSIONS OF ECONOMIC INTEGRATION

The responsibilities for the international trading system have been divided among the World Bank, the IMF, the World Trade Organization (WTO) and the trade-related organizations of the United Nations. These multilateral organizations have developed complex bureaucratic structures and institutional jurisdictions.[17] Since the formation of the GATT in 1947, the United States has taken the lead among nations to create an open, less restrictive trading system. The related social dimensions of economic integration have been the task mainly of the International Labor Organization, which was reshaped at the ILO Conference in Philadelphia, 1944, when delegates from 41 countries representing employers, workers and governments, agreed on a new direction for the organization. The Declaration of Philadelphia stated the basic principles that the ILO was committed to:

> First, that it must be the central aim of national and international policy to achieve conditions in which all men and women can pursue their material well-being and their spiritual development in freedom and dignity, economic security, and equal opportunity; and second, that all national and international efforts should be judged in the light of whether or not they help to further this aim.[18]

Despite the seeming convergence of interests between the stated aim of the international finance organizations and the ILO, linkages between the WTO, IMF, the World Bank and the ILO are tenuous at best and non-existent in many respects. The failure to link trade with labor standards and human rights in a meaningful way is understandable in light of the historic growth rates of industrial countries during the period following World War II. The spillover effects of expanding economic activity benefited workers, employers and governments in the Western, developed countries during the 30 years of the 'American Century', muting protests and social disorder. As economic growth slowed in the mid-1970s the Bretton Woods consensus began to crack.

The response in the United States to these changes has taken the form of pursuing perceived violators of the Bretton Woods pact on a unilateral basis and formally linking US economic aid to developing countries with minimal labor standards. Since 1983, the United States has adopted several pieces of trade and international economic legislation that link trade and other economic benefits to a foreign country's labor law and practice. Among these are:

- the 1984 Caribbean Basin Economic Recovery Act,
- the 1984 extension of the Generalized System of Preferences – the rules that provide for most-favored-nation status,
- the 1985 re-authorization of the Overseas Private Investment Corporation,
- the authorization of US participation in the Multilateral Investment Guarantee Agency in 1987, and
- the 1988 Omnibus Trade and Competitiveness Act.

The 1988 Trade Act strengthened the provisions of Section 301 of the Trade Act of 1974, which (a) established in law retaliatory measures against countries found restricting US exports and (b) defined the denial of internationally recognized worker rights as an unfair labor practice. The 1988 Trade Act makes the improvement of worker rights around the world a 'priority objective of US trade policy and increases the demand on executive branch reporting on the status of worker rights abroad'.[19]

The consequences of unilateral action that is provided in these pieces of legislation, especially in the so-called Super 301 provisions of the 1988 Trade Act, pose grave difficulties for adherents to the Bretton Woods system of universal free trade. The 'aggressive unilateralism' of the United States has critics on both sides of the issue: free traders who think the market acts best in an unfettered manner, and labor and human rights advocates who argue that the measures in US law need more aggressive implementation.[20] With the increasing integration of economies and societies in North America which the NAFTA will speed up, these issues will become increasingly polarized unless formal, effective multilateral mechanisms are put into place to deal with the social dimensions of trade and investment. As Jagdish Bhagwati has noted:

> The greatest danger today is that regional free trade areas will multiply, with high-tariff or high-trade barrier countries (for example, Argentina) being embraced by other countries (for example, the United States), causing trade diversion that will harm world efficiency and also harm other GATT members, whose trade will be diverted to less efficient members of the free trade area.[21]

The disparities between social and economic standards in the United States and Mexico, let alone other countries in this hemisphere who are awaiting the outcome of NAFTA, will cause significant trade and investment transfers by businesses in the United States and Canada to the detriment of workers in those countries. Figures 2.2 and 2.3 below give two indications of the vast differences between the skill level of workers, measured in mean years of schooling of the population older than 24 years,

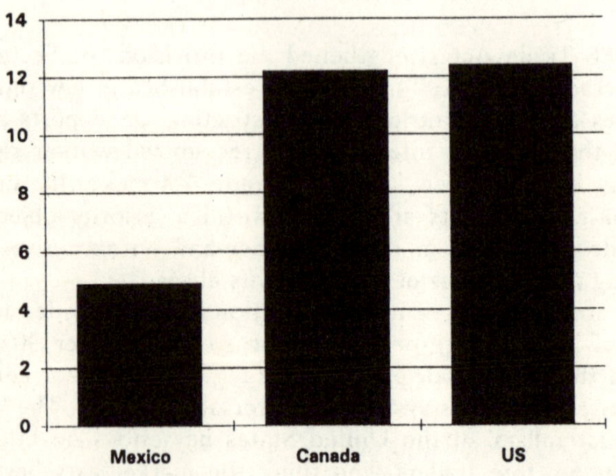


Figure 2.2: Workforce Skill Level (in mean years of schooling).

Source: United Nations Development Programme (1994), Tables 5 and 32, pp. 138 and 188.

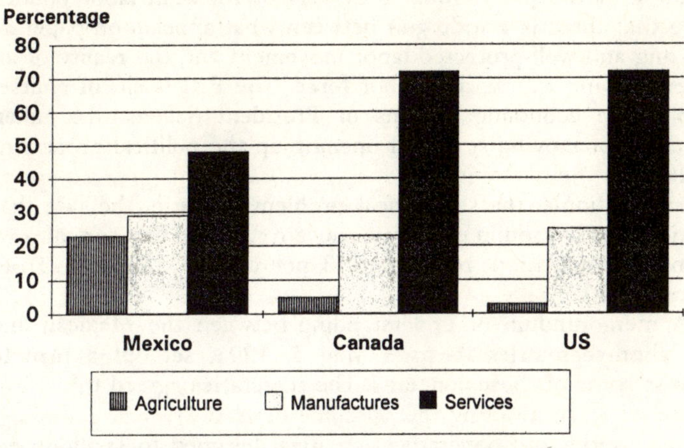


Figure 2.3: Sectoral Labor Force Structure (as percentage of labor force, 1990–92)

Source: United Nations Development Programme (1994), Tables 17 and 38, pp. 162 and 194.

and the sectoral labor force structure of the economies in the United States, Canada and Mexico.

The new trading regime must recognize the gulf between social structures and economic standards that are reflected in these two figures, the limits of relying on market mechanisms to distribute fairly the gains of increasing trade, and the need for democratic participation in determining a social agenda for addressing disparities and inequities in civil society. Such an ambitious agenda can only be achieved through a consensus-building process that includes representatives from business, labor and government in the three countries. This consensus-building process has to start from the shared recognition of facts, not from ideological positions. When President Bush stated that 'Mexico has strong laws regulating labor standards and worker rights',[22] he clearly had divorced himself from the world of facts and gone into the realm of wishful thinking. Laws may indeed look strong on paper, but it is the enforcement of laws through regulatory mechanisms and the acceptance of social norms that we must analyze. The labor movement in Mexico has played the role of an adjunct to the Institutional Revolutionary Party (PRI) since the founding of the party. Most observers of Mexican labor politics agree that there is a wide gulf between what appears on paper as a strong and well-protected labor movement and the reality of an underpaid and overworked labor force. The PRI itself, of course, despite the economic reforms of President Salinas, has taken criticism for moving slowly in opening up the political process in Mexico.[23]

In addition to these political problems there is the fact that Mexico's underground economy, those outside of any sort of governmental regulation, rose from 13 per cent in 1986 to 23 per cent in 1990.[24]

A memorandum of understanding between the Mexican and US labor secretaries released May 3, 1991, set out a plan to address some of these concerns. The secretaries agreed to

> ... a series of cooperative activities designed to facilitate exchanges of information on health and safety, working conditions, labor standards enforcement, labor-management conflict resolution, collective bargaining agreements, social security, credit institutions, labor statistics, and quality and productivity.[25]

While the intention of the exchange of information on these vital topics is certainly a necessary one, it is not sufficient to deal adequately with the consequences of integrating economic activities. As with the WTO, universal rules enforced by law are needed.

The NAFTA labor side agreement negotiated by President Clinton marginally improved the limited idea of information exchange. A new US government institution, the National Administrative Office (NAO) and equivalent institutions in Canada and Mexico, were set up to enforce the labor side agreement. Considering that the NAO was described by one Labor Department insider as little more than a phone and fax machine, its effectiveness will need to be demonstrated.[26]

By involving multilateral organizations in regional economic integration three objectives can be achieved: (a) the principle of universality is maintained; (b) WTO or ILO conventions have the force of an international treaty in the United States, which means that these conventions or standards have the force of law, and (c) the international organizations have well-established mechanisms for building consensus among the various social partners and for resolving disputes between countries.

NAFTA provided a challenge to policymakers from the three countries in business, labor and government. The importance of a successful process for consensus building can hardly be overstated. If two highly developed countries like the United States and Canada can establish a free trade agreement with its less developed neighbor to the south that increases trade and investment opportunities, then other similar agreements surely will follow. In order to achieve the virtuous cycle that is envisioned in this free trade scenario, recognition of the need for a fair and equitable distribution of gains is needed.

## CONCLUSION

The proposal put forward here is that the active role of international organizations, particularly the ILO, WTO, IMF and the World Bank, is needed both to ensure that the interests of all the social partners are represented, and to further ensure that the principles of universalism do not give way to regional blocs of free trade islands that restrict access to non-bloc members. The exact form of coordination that these international organizations would play needs further elaboration. Briefly, here is one way NAFTA could serve as a proving ground for the new WTO in the logical outgrowth of coordinated work between these organizations.

The ILO, IMF, World Bank and WTO would establish an office to coordinate activities for the NAFTA countries and provide a dispute resolution system. Lending policies would be coordinated with the promotion of progressive labor relations systems; macroeconomic policies would seek long-term social adjustment and full employment as well as control of inflation and reduction of indebtedness; growth policies would be promoted along with distributional policies.

Breaking down the institutional barriers between the international organizations, and streamlining the overgrown bureaucracies that have clogged the arteries of these organizations, would be important by-products of establishing an active regional trade organization that is based on universal principles. Creating a mechanism for managing the process of economic integration is a top priority in the world today, whether for Eastern Europe or North America. The sketch provided here outlines an approach that recognizes national sovereignty, universal principles and the need for representing the interests of less powerful social groups in the rush to open markets. Recognizing the social dimensions of economic integration and adopting universal mechanisms are important steps in making sure that the virtuous cycle envisioned emerging out of reducing trade barriers does not become a vicious one based on greed, exploitation and the protection of parochial regional interests against the welfare of all.

This is admittedly only a sketch. There is, however, an acute need for new institutional arrangements that recognize and respond to the increasing social and economic integration, as has occurred over the last 20 years, and which will surely increase now that the ideological battle of the Cold War is over. The unequal distribution of economic gains detailed in this chapter will likely become more pronounced if strong institutions are not erected to protect the interests of workers and citizens as the rush to trade liberalization takes place. In the 1930s a US Senator from New York, Robert F. Wagner, saw a similar situation and proposed a framework that provided for a more balanced relationship between labor and business. In defending his plan Senator Wagner said:

> When wages sink to low levels, the decline in purchasing power is felt upon the marts of trade. [S]ince collective bargaining is the most powerful single force in maintaining and advancing wage rates, its repudiation is likely to intensify the maldistribution of buying power, thus reducing standards of living, unbalancing the economic structure, and inducing depression.[27]

Speaking before the ILO's Conference in 1991, Michel Camdessus, Managing Director of the IMF, cautiously echoed Senator Wagner's words:

> Structural adjustment programmes and programmes of transition to market economies must have social components (nowadays they are called safety nets) that are as complete as possible ... No one is in a better position than the ILO to help establish many of the needed new structures, such as mechanisms for encouraging social dialogue and building tripartite consensus.[28]

The coordination of multilateral activities, like the linking of lending with worker rights or the building of infrastructure to support future economic growth, could serve the critical need of addressing the social dimension of increased economic integration. The challenge to business, labor and government in North America is to move beyond sloganeering to a more coherent, coordinated approach that recognizes that markets are social creations that require managing in order to function properly in the long run. The establishment of a full-time commission, with organizations from appropriate multilateral organizations along with US, Canadian and Mexican representatives from business, labor and government, empowered with financial resources and enforcement authority, is essential to making the process of economic integration work in regional and global trade agreements.

## NOTES

1. Committee for the Promotion of Investment in Mexico, *An Overview of the Maquiladora Industry in Mexico* (Washington, DC: Committee on Economic Development, January 1990).
2. 'Free-Trade Accord Is Enticing Canadian Companies to U.S.', *New York Times*, August 9, 1991, p. A1.
3. United States International Trade Commission (USITC), *The Likely Impact on the United States of a Free Trade Agreement With Mexico*, Publication 2353 (Washington, DC: USITC, 1991).
4. United Nations Development Programme (UNDP), *Human Development Report 1991* (New York: Oxford University Press, 1991) pp. 152 and 186.
5. Timothy Koechlin et al., 'Estimates of the Impact of the Free Trade Agreement on Direct U.S. Investment in Mexico', Testimony to the US Trade Representative, Public Hearings on NAFTA, Boston, 1991.
6. As reported in *Labor Relations Week*, July 3, 1991, p. 621.
7. Lawrence Mishel and David Frankel, *The State of Working America* (Washington, DC: Economic Policy Institute, 1990).
8. 'Median Household Income Fell in 1990 as Poverty Rate Rose', in *Labor Relations Week*, October 2, 1991, p. 907.
9. 'The Rich Are Richer – And America May Be The Poorer', *Business Week*, November 18, 1991, p. 85.
10. Rebecca M. Blank and Maria Hanratty, 'Down and Out in North America: Recent Trends in Poverty Rates in the United States and Canada', *Quarterly Journal of Economics*, vol. 107 (February 1992) pp. 233–54.
11. Rebecca Blank, Professor of Economics at Northwestern University, as reported by Jason DeParle, 'In Debate on U.S. Poverty, 2 Studies Fuel an Argument on Who is to Blame', *New York Times*, October 29, 1991, p. A20. See also Blank and Hanratty, 'Down and Out in North America'; and David Card and Richard B. Freeman, 'Small Differences That Matter: Canada vs the United States' in Richard B.

Freeman (ed.), *Working Under Different Rules*, A National Bureau of Economic Research Project Report (New York, Russell Sage Foundation, 1994) pp. 189–22.

12. Richard B. Freeman, 'How Much Has De-Unionization Contributed to the Rise in Male Earnings Inequality?' in S. Danziger and P. Gottschalk (eds) *Uneven Tides: Rising Inequality in America* (New York: Russell Sage Foundation, 1992) p. 143.
13. European Social Fund, 'Social Action Programme', *Bulletin of the Social Community*, no. 10 (1974) pp. 7–10.
14. As quoted in *AFL-CIO Reviews the Issues*, Report no. 54, September, 1991. AFL-CIO stands for 'American Federation of Labor and Congress of Industrial Organizations'. Located in Washington, DC, the AFL-CIO is the main representative of US labor. The AFL-CIO merged in 1955 from the until then two competing organizations, the American Federation of Labor (formed between 1881 and 1886) and the Congress of Industrial Organizations (formed in 1935).
15. See for example, John T. Addison and W. Stanley Siebert, 'The Social Charter of the European Community: Evolution and Controversies', *Industrial and Labor Relations Review*, vol. 44, no. 4 (July 1991) pp. 597–625.
16. See Stephen J. Silvia, 'The Social Charter of the European Community: A Defeat For European Labor', *Industrial and Labor Relations Review*, vol. 44, no. 4 (July 1991) pp. 626–43.
17. For an analysis of the development of the international trading system see Chapter 1 of Raymond Vernon and Debora L. Spar, *Beyond Globalism: Remaking American Foreign Economic Policy* (New York: The Free Press, 1989).
18. David A. Morse, *The Origins and Evolution of the I.L.O. and Its Role in the World Community* (Ithaca, NY: Cornell University, 1969) p. 28.
19. Jorge F. Perez-Lopez, 'Worker Rights in the U.S. Omnibus Trade and Competitiveness Act', *Labor Law Journal*, vol. 41 (April 1990) pp. 222–34. See also Stephen Sleigh, *The International Labor Organization and the Global Economy* (New York: UNA-USA Publications, 1991).
20. See Jagdish Bhagwati, *The World Trading System at Risk* (Princeton, NJ: Princeton University Press, 1991); and F. Ray Marshall, 'Trade-Linked Labor Standards' in Frank J. Macchiarola (ed.), *International Trade: The Changing Role of the Unites States* (New York: Academy of Political Science Press, 1990).
21. Bhagwati, *The World Trading System at Risk*, p. 77.
22. George Bush, Letter to the US Congress, May 1, 1991, on the NAFTA fast-track provision.
23. See for example, 'The Missing Reform in Mexico', *New York Times*, Editorial, August 26, 1991. On the mid-term elections in Mexico the *Times* said, 'Mr. Salinas failed to turn the elections into the triumph they could easily have been. He seems less impassioned about democracy than about economic reform. That's a serious failing, endan-

gering Mexico's international reputation and the permanence of its economic gains.'

24. According to a survey by the Mexican National Chamber of Manufacturing Industries, as reported in the *Wall Street Journal*, October 17, 1991.
25. US Department of Labor, News Release, May 3, 1991, p. 1.
26. The first complaints on labor rights violation involving Mexican workers dismissed by Honeywell, a US-based corporation, were considered to be a test case for assessing the effectiveness of the NAO. However, the ambiguous result of this test case did not provide clear evidence for or against the effectiveness of the NAO.
27. Senator Robert F. Wagner, *Congressional Record*, May 1, 1935, p. 7572.
28. International Labour Conference, Provisional Record, June 10, 1991, pp. 8/1–8/6.

# 3 Underdevelopment After the Uruguay Round: India

*Bernard D'Mello*

## INTRODUCTION

Capitalism on a global scale is a system that engenders islands of wealth in a sea of mass poverty.[1] It is a system that generates widespread degradation with small areas of flourishing civilization. As a consequence, the minority of human beings who live in wealth and luxury endure anomie. It is in such a system that the GATT's Uruguay Round has been completed and the World Trade Organization (WTO) has been adopted.

This chapter discusses the implications of the rules and regulations of the WTO for India. It begins with a description of some important developments of India's economy over the last few decades. It then analyzes the effects of the rules and regulations of the WTO on India's future development. It provides an uncompromising critique of these rules and regulations. The basic point is that the possibility of successful development seems to be ruled out, with Indian economic policy conforming to the WTO's agenda.

## SOME IMPORTANT DOMESTIC DEVELOPMENTS

The stagnation of the Indian economy over the twentieth century has been well documented by Nirmal Chandra,[2] the principal factor being that the masses remain poverty-stricken which keeps the size of the domestic market far below its potential, especially the market for industrial goods.

Since the early 1960s, the Green Revolution has led to significant increases in output per acre, but per capita increases have been marginal. To develop the agricultural economy further and to realize a greater profit from the surplus, the Indian agrarian ruling groups are turning more towards commercial crops and basmati rice, food processing and the export market. The movement of this class in the relatively advanced regions seems to be from rich peasant to capitalist farmer.[3] The Shetkari Sanghatana, an organization in Maharashtra State led by capitalist farmers, is the principal proponent of this path. The transnational corporations (TNCs), a hitherto despised foreign bourgeoisie, have suddenly become their saviors.[4]

Within the factory sector of Indian industry, projections on employment suggest a gloomy picture. Indeed, it is worse than in the colonial period of this century. The capital output ratio in manufacturing has increased along with the capital labor ratio accompanied by a sluggish expansion of employment opportunities, though with some increase in real earnings.[5] This is an alarming situation, since it implies that (a) income distribution is getting further skewed in the industrial sector, and (b) the gap between the purchasing power of the industrial employees and industrial output is widening.[6]

The managers of the corporate-like state stepped in to relieve the resultant demand constraint within the sector, especially in the 1980s, by increasing expenditures for public administration and defense. This implied an increase in real incomes of public sector and government employees (including the lower-middle income groups). Data for the non-factory small and cottage industries is not reliable. Nevertheless, evidence points to the bulk of expansion in employment having taken place in this low-paid 'informal sector'. Also, the service sector has grown much faster than the national economy in this century. Overall, employment opportunities have slackened significantly in the 1980s.[7]

The 1980s have been heralded as the decade of overcoming what the economist, Raj Krishna, called the 'Hindu rate' of GDP growth (3.4 per cent during 1950–80).[8] But the economic crisis since 1990 seems to have again betrayed hopes of a 'structural break'. Indeed, claims of a 'structural break' can only be hollow for an economy that has failed to provide the basic minimum needs (food, clothing and shelter) of the vast majority of its population.

### *Poverty and Inequality*

Today, India is characterized by mass poverty, misery and degradation in the midst of multi-star hotels, luxurious restaurants, shopping arcades, apartment blocs, Western-style Madison Avenue-type advertising of up-scale consumer products and financial instruments. Poverty, in the official poverty estimates, is defined in terms of a minimum calorie intake apart from a very modest expenditure on non-food items other than education and health which are supposed to be provided to the poor by the state. Recently, the government's Planning Commission has claimed a significant, indeed, a sharp reduction of the rural population living below the poverty line from 37 per cent in 1983/84 to 29 per cent in 1987/88.

This official claim has been strongly contested by independent scholars.[9] After examining various estimates, Nirmal Chandra concludes that the 1987–88 poverty ratio was certainly lower than in the 1970s without crossing the threshold of the early 1960s.[10] The rural poverty ratio for 1987–88 is realistically put at 46.9 per cent which is 12.9 per cent above the 1961–62 level.[11] Assuming that 74.3 per cent of the total population was rural in 1987–88 (the same as in the 1991 census), this implies that 277 million people alone in rural India have not even a minimum food intake in terms of cereals!

The inequalities of income and wealth cannot be reliably estimated but with the increase in the savings rate of the household sector and impressionistic evidence of accumulating ownership of physical capital assets, it seems that income and wealth distribution have become more skewed in favor of the rich. The Indian business class has tempered the growth of real wages, or, at least, real wages have grown modestly in the registered manufacturing sector in the 1980s.[12] Impressionistic evidence also points to a callous attitude in regard to working conditions. There also seems to be a trend of subcontracting to low-wage business units. There is now evidence of a significant fall in unionization in registered manufacturing from 45 per cent of workers unionized in the late 1970s to around 30 per cent in the late 1980s.[13] After taking into account the declining share of workers in registered manufacturing and structural changes within registered manufacturing towards smaller-sized establishments, there is unambiguous evidence of a decline in the strength of organized labor in the 1980s.

Proliferation of slums and pavement dwelling is a symptom of systemic failure. One estimate suggests that in Bombay around 55 per cent of the population of 11 million persons dwell in slums or on the pavements and another 25 per cent in squalid and dilapidated *chawls* (shelters) and buildings.[14] Indeed, even safe sanitation and drinking water are only in meager supply in many places. In the context of globalization, it is also necessary to mention the speculation bubble in real estate prices in major cities, especially Bombay. The plan to locate an international financial center there and allowing foreign capital into real estate in the country may further exacerbate the problem of urban poverty.

Rural poverty and inequality are nothing new. But the new contributing factors, which are seldom discussed, include:

- widespread rigging of elections in rural India, thereby ensuring the continuation of control of the political process by vested interests;
- crushing of movements of landless laborers, poor peasants and forest dwellers by the repressive arms of the state (especially in parts of Bihar and Andhra Pradesh);
- environmental harm caused by surface and ground water pollution, excess top-soil erosion, deforestation and monoculture practices in forestry, desertification, water logging, salinization and water scarcity;[15]
- crisis in the official rural credit system as a result of financial liberalization and financial fraud;
- lesser priority in government expenditure levels and allocation for agriculture and related infrastructure,[16] and
- unsuccessful land reform, which has in some areas not even led to the restoration of common lands (*gair mazarua khas*) presently under the control of a particular owner (*malik*).

Inequality is a wider concept than merely its economic dimension would suggest. There are such attributes as income and wealth but also status, power, knowledge, etc. which are unequally distributed among individuals, families, social groups (gender, caste, tribe, etc.), communities, regions and nations. Economic inequality is rooted in exploitation. In capitalism, however, the other dimensions like status and power, which derive from the individualistic acquisitive drive created by the capitalistic system, are acquired through atomistic competition and coercive means. Knowledge itself is acquired as part of an atomistic competitive process that eliminates many people from childhood, indeed, from birth onwards. India's 'rank' of 135 in a 'countdown' of 173 nations in terms of an index of human development indicators in the UNDP's *Human Development Report 1994* is itself a reflection of the above at the global level.

*Exports*

Two official committees of the 1980s, the Tandon Committee (1980) and the Hussain Committee (1984) endorsed the mainstream view that a 'quantum jump' in exports was possible for and through modernization of the production system via import liberalization. The question of lags between the initial rush of imports and the subsequent flow of exports was to be managed by capital inflow.[17] Indian labor-intensive manufactures, like textiles and garments (see below), face the negative consequences of the politics of international relations rather than the economics of international competition. For reasons other than the above, the Indian corporate sector has fared miserably on the export front despite the government's myriad deregulations and concessions (including export subsidies).[18] Agricultural commodity exports have been liberalized in the 1993–94 trade policy. Capitalist farmers with a significant marketable surplus are very enthusiastic about the Uruguay Round accords on agriculture. They are expecting higher prices from the export market. But what about the price elasticities of agricultural commodity outputs? Will the change in relative prices between different agricultural commodities shift the pattern of output (through substitution) against food crops (sugarcane and oil seeds)? Will there be an increasingly adverse relative price structure between food grains and industrial consumer products in the consumption basket of the poor? In the context of increasing income inequality this may further exacerbate the demand constraint for manufactures.[19]

*The Capital Equipment Sector*

India has one of the most diversified machinery manufacturing sectors in the Third World. But liberalization of technology imports in the 1980s dampened the propensity for local research and development (R&D) relative to technology imports in the machinery sector. Technology imports largely substituted for local R&D. A recent study of India's engineering industry corroborates this with data of payments for technology imports to local R&D expenditure.[20] Conventional wisdom is that the Indian capital goods sector is inefficient and not internationally price competitive.[21] Paradoxically it is a World Bank study which found a number of positive features in a sample of the Indian machinery sector for cement, chemical, pulp and paper and sugar manufacturing machinery, as well as boilers for power plants.[22] Since the 1992–93 union budget, import tariffs on project and general machinery have been coming down from an average of 85 per cent in 1991–92 to 25 per cent in 1994–95. Further, due to high import tariffs on steel and other inputs, the effective rates of protection are even lower than the nominal rates of protection.

### *Finance*

In the jargon of mainstream economics, the Indian financial sector was 'repressed' due to controls on interest rates by government, an over-valued exchange rate, insufficient development of financial institutions, restrictions on money and capital markets, etc. It is argued by the mainstream of the economics profession that all these controls, administered by the government, restricted entry to the market. By keeping finance 'shallow', Indian economic growth was restricted. With such a premise, the Narasimhan Committee's recommendations were predictable: liberalize the financial markets and particularly interest rates.[23] The formal agricultural credit network, created in 1975, now seems to be under severe constraints with increasing deregulation of the banking sector. In the last three years there has been a preference for financial instruments rather than physical investments, especially since real interest rates have been high. Financial investments seem to have offered higher rates of return than physical investments according to recent financial data of non-financial corporations published by the Centre for Monitoring the Indian Economy.

The Indian securities market has witnessed a fantastic growth during 1975–94. Wealthy individuals and corporations increased their wealth by speculating on the stock markets, without 'working' for it. The rash speculation by both wealthy individuals and financial institutions, followed by collapse when the recent financial fraud became public, had some disturbing effects on the economy.

More recently foreign portfolio investment has been an attractive method of inflow of foreign equity capital from non-bank institutional investors. This can help local firms to reduce their debt equity ratios, though there are limits on the proportion of a firm's equity capital which may be foreign-owned. This latter stipulation is to prevent control passing into foreign hands which Indian industrialists fear can happen.[24] The other problem is the volatility of foreign portfolio investment.

With the breakdown of the Bretton Woods fixed exchange-rate arrangement in the early 1970s and the burgeoning current account deficits of the underdeveloped countries, the transnational banks have slowly but surely moved in with their international network of recycling finance over the globe. Bank lending was reduced to a trickle after India became a serious risk country for the transnational banks on the Euro-market (see for example India's poor credit rating by Moody's in early 1992).[25] India though has been an ambivalent borrower for the transnational banks. But the source of the debt problem, even for a country like India with considerable inflows of foreign direct investment (FDI) and external borrowing, may be the recurring outflows of dividends and interest when viewed in the long term.[26] Short-term flows of finance (though difficult to track) can be destabilizing, for together these can be around 20–25 per cent of total lending. In 1990 and 1991 India faced such a situation – a bunching of repayments of amortization and interest. Foreign direct investment has not been buoyant, though the flows improved after July 1991. FDI seems to be more for exploiting the Indian market in manufactured goods than for export.[27]

The build-up of foreign exchange reserves in the last year is the result of poor utilization of net private capital inflow. According to one estimate hardly 15 per cent of the funds collected from Euro-issues have been earmarked for financing new projects. The bulk are used for repaying past loans (taken at much higher interest rates) or to acquire real estate.[28]

With priority being assigned to agricultural exports, India might come to depend on a narrow range of commodity exports (especially rice and cotton) thus leading to a greater variability of exports earnings. Indeed the World Bank's structural adjustment program (SAP), if carried to its logical end, can lead the economy back to being less diversified. Then, if the impact of the specific risk factors (variability of export earnings) coincides with the cyclical impact of systematic risk (the cyclical downturn in the advanced capitalist economies), there may be a severe fall in export earnings, worsening India's debt-servicing capacity. The impact can be worse than hitherto with the dismantling of controls on trade, production, investment, prices, interest rates and the exchange rate. A terms-of-trade deterioration then would be disastrous.

Stabilization and structural adjustment have been the common prescription of Fund/Bank medicine for faltering Third

World economies. The stabilization package, like the original Polak model, is broadly monetarist.[29] The IMF's 'seal of approval' was necessary to reopen the gates for Indian corporations (public enterprises and private) to tap the Euro-market. The Fund has thus played its role as the catalyst and can now take a back seat for a while. But the Fund/Bank prescription of the simultaneous policy instruments of import liberalization and reduction of the fiscal deficit (more specifically, targeting public investment) has been an 'overkill', putting the economy into a severe recession. This attempt to combine the stabilization program with the SAP is particularly troubling. However, the government leaders will be forced to 'go slow' (stop-go-stop) under popular pressure. Indeed, indications are that the 'go slow' has already begun. But the ominous implications of the Uruguay Round for India's economy have been sinking in and are analyzed below.

## LIKELY IMPACT OF THE URUGUAY ROUND

From the point of view of transnational capital, the adoption of the Uruguay Round's results brought on a new agenda to the international management of the world economy. New accords on trade-related intellectual property rights (TRIPs), trade-related investment measures (TRIMs), and trade in services will be incorporated into the WTO system of rights and obligations. The WTO was established to bring about more coherent institutional links (from the viewpoint of the triad of the United States, the European Community and Japan) between itself, the IMF and the World Bank. One now wonders how Article XVIII (b) of GATT, which permits an 'infant industry' protection so long as a country has balance-of-payments problems, will be compatible with the Fund/Bank's stabilization and SAPs, especially the latter which stipulate import liberalization. This is going to be a controversial point. However, the institutional linkages between the WTO on the one hand, and the Fund/Bank on the other, have not yet been established legally. There is also apprehension about the possible annexation of areas like environment, investment, competition policy, etc. from the national realm.[30] One point that has not been stressed but which requires attention is the whole problem of cross-retaliation between trade in goods and services sectors, interlinking patents, copyrights and trademarks.[31]

### International Trade in Food

The agricultural community in an advanced capitalist country often has sufficient political influence to protect its business interests from the devastating effects of the market. Agricultural exports from the European Community (EC) have competed strongly in world markets with agricultural exports from the United States and Cairns Group countries. Often, agricultural surpluses are virtually dumped on world markets with adverse consequences for the Third World countries' exports of farm commodities. Third World countries may be lower cost producers due to low wages and conducive natural factors (tropical climates) but lose these advantages to the European Community because of the latter countries' farm-sector support schemes.

While the Cairns Group loses due to the European Community's farm policy, Japan subsidizes its agricultural sector (perhaps even more than the European Community) purely for the domestic market (mainly to maintain food security of rice). Japan protects its farmers through severe quantitative restrictions on imports because the world market mechanism could ruin Japanese agriculture. The problem has been settled by political means and not by the market. What has been agreed to in the GATT accord on agriculture is essentially a compromise on improved market access, domestic support reduction and export subsidy reduction.

### Biotechnology in the Farm Sector

This issue seems to be an important bone of contention as was evident in the mass turn-out at a rally on October 2 (the birthday of Mahatama Gandhi), 1993, organized by the Karnataka Rajya Rayat Sangh (KRRS) and the Karnataka Farmers Association led by M.D. Nandgundaswamy.[32] The KRRS had earlier targeted the premises of the TNC Cargill. The issue has however larger implications. There is a need for a clear understanding of the technological evolution of the agro-food system.

One set of advances is replacing Third World producers' crops. For example, sugar from sugarcane is being replaced by high-fructose corn syrup. Another set of innovations, which use carbohydrates as the feedstock, can increase the demand for cassava and potato. Therefore, the application of biotechnology (and genetic engineering) has mixed results.[33] Critics have complained of a growing loss of genetic diversity.[34] On the other hand, the claims made by some agricultural scientists, including Indian scientist M.S. Swaminathan,[35] for hybrid seed-based crops seems highly exaggerated. Biotechnology has been falsely 'marketed' as a panacea for the Third World's food problems.[36]

Indian agriculture is on the way to being significantly affected by bio-technology in the coming decades, given the interest shown both by the transnational hybrid seed companies and a section of capitalist farmers. But, most likely, just as the Green Revolution led to 'big gains in little areas', the same is likely to be the fate of the new hybrid varieties. However, hybrid seeds for cotton and especially oil seeds and pulses can be particularly beneficial, especially the former two, given the fact that there is a dire need for a breakthrough in the growth of output of these crops.

A number of cautions need to be mentioned:

- The original developments, of, say, hybrid corn, were in non-profit public institutions, but private transnational capital directs much of the present research in hybrid seeds.[37]

- The hybrid seeds are said to be reproductively unstable, thereby forcing farmers to purchase seeds annually or at the time of planting/sowing. It would be ominous for a country like India if it had to import these seeds or if this seed supply were controlled by transnational affiliates/subsidiaries in India.[38]

- The planting of these seeds can lead to loss of genetic diversity and increased vulnerability of crops to pests.[39]

- The basic feedstocks are in India and this may attract a number of TNCs in seed production and multiplication to come to India. The local availability of feedstocks, as well as the quality of Indian scientific talent, can be seized upon by the agricultural research institutes. Indeed, biotechnology and applied genetic engineering research can be made a growth area with high priority in India for these very reasons.[40]

- The success of hybrid seed-based crops depends on petrochemical fertilizers and pesticides, the latter linked to particular varieties of seeds.[41]

The hybrid seed agrochemical combinations are themselves marketed by related firms of the same transnational group. Another point which needs to be reiterated is that, under the Plant Breeder Rights granted in Europe, farmers can multiply proprietary seeds for sowing in their own fields but not for sale. The breeders however acquire the rights to royalties from farmers multiplying seeds for their own use. Hence, the KRRS in India has rightly taken a strong stand against effective *sui generis* or a patenting system for hybrid seeds. In fact, a 1993 draft of a Plant Varieties Act, circulated by the Indian government, provides heightened protection in Plant Breeders Rights as provided in the 1991 amendments of the 1978 International Convention for the Protection of New Varieties of Plants. Also, the draft act ignores the UN Convention on Biological Diversity that seeks to give developing countries the benefits of the R&D in biotechnology carried out with germplasms obtained from them.[42]

### *Trade-Related Intellectual Property Rights (TRIPs)*

India instituted a 'nationalistic' Indian Patents Act (IPA) in 1970 to replace the old colonial act of 1911 against much opposition from the representatives of the TNCs in the pharmaceutical and agrochemical industry.[43] The term of patents in the 1970 IPA is five years from the date of sealing the patent or seven years from the filing of complete specifications (whichever is shorter) in the case of foods, pharmaceuticals, veterinary products, pesticides and agrochemicals. For products other than these the term is 14 years from the date of filing complete specifications.[44]

Section 5 of the IPA permits only process patents protection in the above-mentioned industries. There are no patents permitted in the areas of biotechnology and environmental pollution control. There are provisions for compulsory licensing (Section 84 (2)) and licenses of right (Section 87 (1)). The latter entitles an aspiring business to be granted a license to manufacture a patented product or use a patented process if the patentee does not exploit his/her patent within a stipulated period of time. Importation is not sufficient to establish that a patent is being exploited. Sections 2(h) and 99 entitle the government including a 'government undertaking' to use a patent for its 'own use'.

Chaudhury cites a number of cases where Indian pharmaceutical manufacturers have worked around the process to produce the same product, partly through imitation or through the development of alternative process technologies.[45] This upset the innovators' (usually a TNC) monopoly or quasi-monopoly position, increased the supply of the drug in question and placed the offer price under a downward pressure. Thus the IPA 1970 has, in certain cases, undermined the monopoly position of the TNCs. The latter have been decrying this, saying it upsets the incentive to invest in R&D.

The TRIPs accord will negate the advantage that consumers and competing producers derived from the IPA 1970, for the latter will have to be virtually scrapped *in toto*:

- Section 5 of the IPA 1970 will have to be amended because of Article 70.8 (1) of the TRIPs accord.

- India will have to provide five-year exclusive marketing rights to pharmaceutical and agrochemical producers for which product patents have been filed (Article 70.9 of the TRIPs accord).

- From 1999, the exclusions from patents for plants and animals and biotechnological processes for the production of plants and animals as well as plant varieties will be reviewed (Article 27.3 of TRIPs).

- India must provide effective *sui generis* protection of plant varieties by 2000 AD (Article 65.1, Article 65.2).

- India must start the process of granting patents for product patent applications filed after 1995 for pharmaceutical and agrochemicals by 2000 AD (Article 70.8 (ii)).

- By 2000 AD India must grant 20-year process patents and product patents (the latter for products other than pharmaceutical and agrochemicals) and conform to the TRIPs provisions including the one that the burden of proof of innocence will lie with the accused (Articles 65.1, 65.2 and 70.8). Truly, in this context, the latter flies in the face of modern jurisprudence or even the basic principles of Roman law!

- India must grant product patents for pharmaceutical and agrochemicals from the filing date for 20 years thereafter (Article 65.4; 70.8 (iii)).

Importation will be equivalent to the working of a patent locally, thus discouraging local production, increasing foreign exchange outflows, reducing employment and increasing prices.[46] TRIPs stipulate that countries shall provide protection for plant varieties by patents or by an effective *sui generis* system or any combination thereof. Hopefully the contradictions of commercial interest between the United States and European Community will delay the schedule of commitment element of the accord. The US Supreme Court was the first to grant a patent for a micro-organism (to Anand Chakavarty of the University of Chicago in 1980). The inclusion of genes as micro-organisms means that a patent granted on a transgenic construct will automatically translate into a patent on that particular plant or animal.[47]

Manipulation of genetic material has become a routine method since 1982 and has led to tremendous advances in the pharmaceutical, agricultural and industrial biotechnology based areas. In Sahai's view, 'India could emerge as a global player in biotechnology if it was not hamstrung by an inequitable patent system [such as the TRIPs accord] totally out of touch with its requirements.'[48]

### *Trade-Related Investment Measures (TRIMs)*

TRIMs have applied GATT Article III on national treatment and GATT Article XI on prohibiting the use of quantitative restrictions to regulations regarding foreign investment. The advanced capitalist countries regard targets specified for local content and export performance for foreign investment as trade barriers, hence the application of GATT principles to regulation of foreign investment. Countries like India applied these regulations on foreign investment for trade balancing purposes. 'National treatment' will now require treating domestic and imported inputs equally. However, subsidies can be given to domestic producers and preferences for locally manufactured goods can be applied to government procurement (the 'Buy America' Act is therefore in conformity with the GATT provision).

India can no longer apply the so-called Phased Manufacturing Program (PMP) clause to limit an enterprise's source of inputs to local manufactures or limit the purchase of imported inputs linked to the value of local production the enterprise exports. Of course, India had largely done away with the Phased Manufacturing Program in 1991. However, in the wake of the foreign exchange crisis in 1991, India's foreign direct investment policy had specified certain limits on repatriation of dividends linked to net foreign exchange earnings of the enterprise (India later scrapped this provision). The point, however, is that India cannot now resort to policy measures of this kind should a balance-of-payments crisis occur again. It seems that India will not be permitted even to apply a restriction on access of an enterprise to foreign exchange if that foreign exchange has been earned by the enterprise, even in the event of a balance-of-payments crisis. The only concession, if this is construed as one, is that the last date by which a country like India will be required to eliminate all TRIMs is 2000 AD. But, India has, for all practical purposes, already fallen in line with TRIMs.

### *Textiles and Clothing*

Textiles and clothing are products that are 'labor intensive' and hence 'free trade' is to the advantage of Third World exporters. In fact India was the largest developing country exporter of textiles in 1958–59. However, GATT principles have not applied to this sector. This is because the advanced capitalist countries with textile industries had to undergo 'structural adjustment' in this sector.

The Multi-Fibre Arrangement (MFA) has led to non-uniform treatment of developing countries, favoring some at the expense of others. Developing countries which were allotted big quotas have been able to sell their products at high prices in the industrialized countries, something that would not have been possible if the forces of competition had been given full sway. Developing countries that were not textile exporters prior to 1962 were virtually shut off, thus barring their entry into the export market.

It is truly amazing that the MFA has lasted for 34 years and has been given another ten years to be phased out. It is expected that over the next decade the further introduction of microcontrollers (the blue-collar equivalent of the white-collar microprocessors) in textile machinery will facilitate the shift of textiles and clothing manufacturing back to the industrialized countries. Already, with open-end spinning techniques and shuttle-less looms, multi-phase looms, double-knitting machines, non-woven fabrics and programmed pattern printing, comparative advantage seems to be shifting back to the industrialized countries.

### *Trade in Services*

For quite some time now, the service sector has become the dominant sector in terms of employment (up to two-thirds of total employment) in the industrialized countries. In terms of technological efficiency, activities like retailing, banking, insurance, securities transactions, transport, communications and tourism, the industrialized countries are way ahead. Many of these services – for example, advertising, banking, insurance, communications, transport – constitute the logistical base for the organization of TNCs at home and abroad. Hence, when the TNCs come to a country like India, they prefer to deal with the same set of market participants as they deal with in their home countries. The financial services industry is particularly advanced in countries like the United States. Besides brokerage services, primary market services in the form of underwriting, syndication, private placement and marketing of new securities are also being infiltrated by foreign firms in India.

For India, besides financial services, trade in services would mainly concern tourism, data processing and communication (a very buoyant activity), audio-visual media, construction and installation, and engineering consultancy services. Because of the simultaneity of production and consumption, most services have to be provided on the spot. Computer software, of course, is provided 'invisibly' via telecommunication networks. With the GATT accord on services, India may have to lift the seal off markets by amending banking and insurance laws. Government monopoly of the telecommunication sector, already partially opened up, may have to give way to equal treatment for all, Indian and foreign businesses. The Centre for the Development of Telematics (C-DOT), an innovative Indian organization in digital telecommunications, together with the network of local manufacturer-suppliers it has helped nurture, are likely to be hurt badly.

Since financial services are locale specific, India may have to provide freedom of capital movements. With advanced technological developments in the form of digitally coded information that can be provided cheaply, quickly and reliably via telecommunication systems, the globalization of the financial sector in India is a real possibility after the Uruguay Round. Already plans are afoot to develop Bombay as an international financial center. India will then witness the entry of several more TNCs in banking, insurance, advertising, tourism, etc. in Bombay. There are escape clauses in the GATT accord on services under which national protection can be sought, but the Indian government now seems to have a bias in favor of the TNCs.

In the final analysis, it has to be admitted that the kind of capital-intensive services provided by the advanced capitalist countries, whether a McDonald's or a Pizza Hut retail outlet network or advanced financial intermediation by a Citicorp, these services are consumed by the very rich. Indeed, all indications are that the income elasticities of demand for such services would be very high at already high levels of incomes by Indian standards. Indeed, these services would cater to demand created only by those upper-income brackets. Employment creation would be negligible, indeed, the intrusion of such business may have a negative employment effect overall.

### *Fair International Trade?*

The Uruguay Round conclusion may witness a reduction of ceiling tariff levels of the Third World to around 30 per cent. But what about non-tariff barriers like the so-called voluntary export restraints (VERs). India is at a disadvantage due to VERs in shoes, steel, low-level machine tools, steel products and auto components. VERs are *de facto* import licenses. There are also many grey-area measures such as unduly high standards stipulated, limited access to public invitations to tender and unnecessary complications in commercial documentation. These affect India since she is otherwise internationally competitive in construction, installation and engineering services.

### *Environmental and Social Clauses*

The support given by the Shetkari Sanghatana in Maharashtra, India, an organization led by rich farmers but with a large middle peasant base, to the GATT accord is myopic. The increasing rape of the natural environment, like deforestation and soil erosion, has to be seen partly as a consequence of the increasing pressure on foreign debt-ridden nations to export. The issue of what is termed 'eco-dumping' – when the choice of location by a TNC in a particular developing country is determined by the virtual *carte blanche* it receives to pollute the environment – is a serious issue in the context of recent decisions to locate a number of chloro-chemical plants in India.

The United States has raised the question of 'social dumping'. The interpretation is that a country or business that violates the labor standards agreed to under the International Labor Organisation (ILO) violates the principles of free trade. Indeed, the US government is backed by the right-wing International Confederation of Free Trade Unions (ICFTU). US law of 1988 empowers the US Department of Commerce to take measures against countries which violate labor practices such as those agreed to under the ILO auspices. Violation of these labor practices are endemic in India. The People's Union for Democratic Rights (PUDR), Delhi has documented the lives and struggles of workers in Bhilai where practically all the labor laws are violated.[49] The US government is raising such issues for safeguarding the pecuniary interests of US business, not out of any genuine concern for the violations of human rights. Indeed, while raising such issues, the US government has never acknowledged the fact or indeed even the existence of people's movements struggling for a better life in these areas.

## CONCLUSION: PUTTING THE STRANDS TOGETHER

The above analysis has shown that the adoption of the Uruguay Round results implies considerable drawbacks for India's development. On the other hand, it benefits the ruling groups in the industrialized countries. These consequences taken together imply that the WTO reinforces long-term stagnation for underdeveloped economies in the system of global capitalism. This does not imply that there are no changes. However, the essential continuity is that the masses will remain poverty-bound and that the Indian market will be constrained by the poor's low purchasing power. Now, with the lowering of protection levels, the possibilities of further import substitution are almost exhausted.

Although the service sector may continue to grow faster than the national economy, the intrusion of capital intensive services is likely to have negative impacts on employment generation. Regional imbalances can be expected to be further exacerbated with the introduction of hybrid seed-based technologies. Since these technologies require access to advanced resource bases, such as irrigation, power, agricultural machinery, fertilizers and pesticides, further diversion of resources to the advanced regions is likely, thereby exacerbating the problems of underdevelopment.

Although India is poverty-stricken, nevertheless, it has created one of the most diversified industrial structures in the Third World. Indeed, certain segments of the capital goods sector and the Indian pharmaceutical industry are potentially internationally competitive.[50] The long-term prospects of Indian textile exports and domestic textile machinery manufacture seem dim. The implementation of the Uruguay Round accords can seriously debilitate the above-mentioned industrial sectors. The forces of agribusiness are slowly entering Indian agriculture via the transition of rich peasants to capitalist farmers, although only in a few areas. With the lid capped on public investment, and given the limits on the fiscal deficit (imposed by the IMF), public infrastructure is decaying.

Excess capacity and unemployment seem endemic. The financial sector is poised to increase its share of India's GDP. When and if the focus of Indian capitalism tilts in favor of the financial sector and against agriculture and industry, the results could be disastrous, for India is still an underdeveloped economy.[51] Already there is some evidence of simultaneous financial prosperity and productive stagnation. The cash-rich corporations, besides putting their cash reserves in marketable securities, are players in the merger and acquisition business.[52] Meanwhile, there is greater clamor for widespread privatization and easy 'exit policy' for bankrupt businesses. The financial liberalization – especially of priority-sector lending (if accompanied by a tendency for real interest rates to increase) may see many more small industrial units bankrupt. And agriculture, which typically needs more working capital than industry because of its long production cycle, will be hit worse by a credit crunch.

The GATT commodity accords will have to be examined carefully to assess the impact on the effective rates of protection (ERP) in the advanced capitalist countries, compared to the ERP in developing countries. This may give a better assessment of relative gains and losses. It seems that some of the declining industries of the industrialized countries (steel, textiles and garments, electronics, shoes, automobiles and machine tools) will enjoy higher ERP after the Uruguay Round. This may mean a real prospect of deepening underdevelopment. Agriculture may also be a strong contender. India's capital goods and pharmaceutical industry may be in deep trouble, the former with low ERP and the latter without protection against monopolistic practices of the TNCs. Indian consumers of pharmaceuticals may also be badly bruised when they have to spend a greater proportion of their consumption baskets on food and pharmaceuticals. The technological dependence of Indian agriculture and industry may indeed be further deepened by the impact of the Uruguay Round accords on the Indian patent system.

If India's capitalist farmers hitch their business prospects with the TNCs in international trade of hybrid seeds and agrochemicals, this may further threaten the food security of India's poor.

Liberal economists are hoping that the export thrust of Indian agriculture may be accompanied by productivity gains, both in yield per acre and in output per worker, to increase the wage rates of the agricultural laborers significantly. It is more likely that such capital-intensive agriculture will result in further rural unemployment, given a 2.2 per cent growth rate of population. Furthermore, environmental and social degradation may also be exacerbated.

The Bretton Woods agreement of 1944 brought the infamous twins – the Fund and Bank – on stage to manage the international economy. The WTO is set to join the twins to become a triad in international management. This triad seems to be set to manage the New World Order of the 1990s on behalf of another triad – the United States, Germany and Japan – with all the inter-imperialist contradictions.

In the same year the Bretton Woods conference took place, a Hungarian scholar, Karl Polanyi, published *The Great Transformation: The Political and Economic Origins of Our Time*.[53] Polanyi radically attacked the market economy as a means of organizing economic life. In his view, the market economy was incapable of meeting the material, social and spiritual needs of people.[54] Polanyi's work describes the efforts of people, backed ultimately by their governments through popular pressures, to protect themselves from the disruptive effects of market forces.[55] Polanyi had a moral abhorrence of capitalism. He had a conviction that it would have to give way to some form of genuine socialism. Vast suffering has been caused to the poor in India where they are presently deprived of even the last vestiges of human dignity as India moves from degenerated national capitalism to neoliberal, peripheral capitalism. This situation can be overcome if and when the struggle of the Indian people for salvaging and safeguarding their democratic rights moves forward. Polanyi had a vision that 'habitat' and 'improvement' can be ensured through social control. The habitability and security of life and individuals in their natural and socio-cultural environments and compatibility of these with productivity and economic growth is thus possible. Polanyi's vision needs to be renewed.

## NOTES

1. Paul A. Baran, *The Political Economy of Growth* (New York: Monthly Review Press, 1957).

2. Nirmal K. Chandra, 'Long-Term Stagnation in the Indian Economy, 1900–75' in Nirmal K. Chandra, *The Retarded Economies* (Bombay: Oxford University Press, 1988) pp. 157–252; Nirmal K. Chandra, 'The New Economic Policy, Stagnation and De-Industrialization', paper presented at a Seminar on New Economic Policy, at the Indian Institute of Management (IIM), Calcutta, August 19–21, 1993.
3. The movement has also been depicted as a movement from rich peasants to capitalist farmers to farmer capitalists, see for example V. Date, 'Shetkari Leaders Venture: Soybean Extraction Unit in Wardha', *The Times of India*, Bombay, August 24, 1993; and A. Mishra, 'Farmers in the Dunkel Draft', *The Times of India*, Bombay, November 14, 1993.
4. Recently, Mr Garland West, a spokesperson of the Minneapolis-based TNC, Cargill, remarked that the views expressed by Professor Nanjundaswamy, one of the leaders of the Karnataka peasants movement against the transnational seed companies, 'are not reflective of the entire farming community', see 'Cargill Plans US$30m Investment' in *The Times of India*, Bombay, October 9, 1993. During the annual convention of the Shetkari Sanghatana (Cargill's political ally) Ajit Narade, a leader from Kolhapur remarked, 'If I meet [Arthur] Dunkel on my way back home, I will pin the Sanghatana's badge on his lapel', see A. Mishra, 'Farmers in the Dunkel Draft', *The Times of India*, Bombay, November 14, 1993. Indeed, the Sanghatana's activists in Kolhapur, led by Ajit Narade, have even gone to the extent of offering land to Cargill to set up base in Kolhapur in view of the attacks the TNC has faced from peasants in Karnataka, see V. Date, 'Shetkari Leaders Venture: Soybean Extraction Unit in Wardha', *The Times of India*, Bombay, August 24, 1993.
5. Chandra, 'Long-Term Stagnation in the Indian Economy 1900–75', p. 174; and R. Nagaraj, 'Employment and Wages in Manufacturing Industries: Trends, Hypothesis and Evidence', *Economic & Political Weekly*, vol. 29, no. 4 (January 22, 1994) pp. 177–86.
6. Chandra, 'Long-Term Stagnation in the Indian Economy 1900–75', p. 172.
7. Official data from the National Sample Survey Organization (NSSO) point to a decline in the quinquennial annual growth rates of employment – 2.8 per cent in 1972/73–1977/78 to 2.2 per cent in 1977/78–1983, and 1.6 per cent in 1983–1987/88. The last quinquennial annual growth rate is a pointer to the dismal situation. Employment expansion is failing to keep pace with the growth rate of population, 2.2 per cent per annum during 1971–1991. The most serious cause for alarm is the precipitous fall in employment growth rates in Indian agriculture from 2.3 per cent in 1972/73–1977/78 to 0.7 per cent in 1983–1987/88. In the manufacturing sector too, the decline is extremely disconcerting – from 5.1 per cent per annum in 1972/73–1977/78 to 2.1 per cent in 1983–1987/88. Much of the growth of employment in the manufacturing sector is in the informal

sector. See Chandra, 'The New Economic Policy, Stagnation and De-Industrialization'.

8. The annual average growth rate of real GDP during 1980–89 was around 5.2 per cent. But the annual percentage growth rates were not significantly better than the earlier corresponding period of rapid growth, 1955–64. The performance of the 1980s isn't exceptional. Indeed, the 1920s witnessed comparable growth rates. See Chandra, 'The New Economic Policy, Stagnation and De-Industrialization', pp. 1–2.
9. See Chandra, 'The New Economic Policy, Stagnation and De-Industrialization', p. 6, with further references.
10. Chandra, 'The New Economic Policy, Stagnation and De-Industrialization', p. 6.
11. Chandra, 'The New Economic Policy, Stagnation and De-Industrialization', p. 6.
12. Nagaraj, 'Employment and Wages in Manufacturing Industries: Trends, Hypothesis and Evidence'.
13. Nagaraj, 'Employment and Wages in Manufacturing Industries: Trends, Hypothesis and Evidence', p. 180.
14. G. Singh, 'Slum Re-Development: Failed Schemes', *The Times of India*, July 4, 1993.
15. Anil K. Agarwal, 'Nature and Society in Modernising India' in C.M. Borden (ed.), *Contemporary India: Essays on the Uses of Tradition* (Delhi: Oxford University Press, 1989).
16. S.L. Shetty, 'Investment in Agriculture: Brief Review of Recent Trends', *Economic & Political Weekly*, vol. 25, nos 7 & 8 (February 17–24, 1990) pp. 389–98; see also the Editorial on 'Investment in Agriculture: Creating Illusions', *Economic & Political Weekly*, vol. 29, no. 27 (July 2, 1994) p. 1620.
17. Nirmal K. Chandra, 'Modernisation for Export-Oriented Growth: A Critique of Recent Indian Policy' in Nirmal K. Chandra, *The Retarded Economies* (Bombay: Oxford University Press, 1988) pp. 339–80.
18. Chandra, 'The New Economic Policy, Stagnation and De-Industrialization', p. 9.
19. For the 1970s, see N. Krishnaji, 'The Demand Constraint: A Note on the Role of Food Grain Prices and Income Inequality' in N. Krishnaji, *Pauperising Agriculture: Studies in Agrarian Change and Demographic Structure* (Bombay: Sameeksha Trust, by Oxford University Press, 1992) pp. 96–109.
20. See Chandra, 'The New Economic Policy, Stagnation and De-Industrialization', p. 11.
21. Sukhamoy Chakravarty, *Development Planning: The Indian Experience* (Oxford: Clarendon Press, 1987).
22. World Bank (1984), as quoted in Chandra, 'Modernisation for Export-Oriented Growth'.
23. Reserve Bank of India (RBI), Narasimhan Committee, *Report of the Committee on the Financial System*; Summary reprinted in *Reserve*

*Bank of India Bulletin*, vol. 46, no. 2 (February 1991) pp. 369–80.

24. N.A. Palkhiwala, a corporate lawyer and luminary of the Indian business scene, recently expressed fears of a change in corporate control in this manner in his annual speech on the 1994–95 Union Budget; see *The Statesman*, March 10, 1994.
25. Moody's Investors Service publishes a comprehensive series of manuals containing key data for business and financial sectors. For example, *Moody's International Manual* provides a wide reference source for financial and business information on approximately 4,700 major corporations, sovereigns and their municipalities, and national and supranational institutions in 108 countries on an annual basis. *Moody's International New Reports* are published every week and include information on interim financial statements, personnel changes, etc.
26. Bernard D'Mello, 'Third World Debt', *Frontier*, vol. 16 (December 10, 1983) pp. 8–11.
27. Sudip Chaudhuri, 'Regulation of the TNCs and the New Economic Policies', paper presented at a Seminar on New Economic Policy, at the Indian Institute of Management (IIM), Calcutta, August 19–21, 1993. Also, mining, food and tobacco, trading, petroleum refining and even electric power generation seem to be attracting the attention of the TNCs, going by the proposals for FDI which have been submitted to the 'fast track' Foreign Investment Promotion Board.
28. This information was provided by Mr Jairam Ramesh, a senior official of India's Planning Commission at a session on 'Foreign Investment and Euro-issues' of a conference organized by the Federation of Indian Chambers of Commerce & Industry at Calcutta, April 29, 1993; see *The Telegraph*, Calcutta, April 30, 1993.
29. Jaques J. Polak, 'Monetary Analysis of Income Formation and Payments Problems', *IMF Staff Papers*, vol. 6, no. 1 (November 1957) pp. 1–50. Of course, there are further developments which incorporate the World Bank's structural adjustment programs (SAPs) and the IMF's stabilization programs into monetarist and supply-side economics' theoretical framework. But the analytical underpinnings are that of the two-gap model and the monetary approach to the balance of payments. See Mohsin S. Khan, Peter J. Montiel and N.U. Haque, 'Adjustment With Growth: Relating the Analytical Approaches of the IMF and the World Bank', *Journal of Development Economics*, vol. 32 (1990) pp. 155–79.
30. S.P. Shukla, 'Resisting the World Trade Organisation: Agenda for Marrakesh', *Economic & Political Weekly*, vol. 29, no. 11 (March 12, 1994) pp. 589–92.
31. For a recent legal interpretation, which was helpful for the author's analysis, see R. Dhawan and A. Vishwanathan, 'Seeds: Concealing the Real Story', *The Times of India*, May 9, 1994; and R. Dhawan and A. Vishwanathan, 'A Guide to the Final GATT Treaty', *Frontline*, vol. 11, no. 9 (May 6, 1994) pp. 123–9.

32. Wishvas Rane, 'Farmers' Rally Against GATT Proposals', *Economic & Political Weekly*, vol. 28, no. 44 (October 30, 1993) pp. 2391–6.
33. David Goodman, Bernardo Sorj and John Wilkinson, *From Farming to Biotechnology* (New York: Basil Blackwell, 1987).
34. Vandana Shiva, 'Farmers' Rights, Biodiversity and International Treaties', *Economic & Political Weekly*, vol. 28, no. 14 (April 3, 1993) pp. 555–60.
35. Monkombu S. Swaminathan, 'Biotechnology and Third World Agriculture', *Science*, no. 218 (December 3, 1982) pp. 967–72.
36. Swaminathan, 'Biotechnology and Third World Agriculture'.
37. M. Kenny, 'Is Biotechnology a Blessing for the Less Developed Nations?', *Monthly Review*, vol. 34, no. 11 (April 1993) pp. 11–19.
38. Kenny, 'Is Biotechnology a Blessing for the Less Developed Nations?'.
39. Shiva, 'Farmers' Rights, Biodiversity and International Treaties'.
40. Suman Sahai, 'GATT and Patenting of Micro Organisms', *Economic & Political Weekly*, vol. 29, no. 15 (April 9, 1994) pp. 841–2.
41. Suman Sahai, 'Patenting of Life Forms: What Does it Imply', *Economic & Political Weekly*, vol. 29, no. 17 (April 9, 1992) pp. 878–9.
42. Dhawan and Vishwanathan, 'Seeds: Concealing the Real Story'.
43. Sudip Chaudhuri, 'Dunkel Draft on Drug Patents: Background and Implications', *Economic & Political Weekly*, vol. 28, no. 36 (September 4, 1993) pp. 1861–5.
44. See sections 53 (1) and 45 (1) of the 1970 Indian Patents Act.
45. Chaudhuri, 'Dunkel Draft'.
46. Chaudhuri, 'Dunkel Draft'.
47. Sahai, 'GATT and Patenting of Micro Organisms', p. 841.
48. Sahai, 'GATT and Patenting of Micro Organisms', p. 842.
49. People's Union for Democratic Rights (PUDR), *Tall Chimneys, Dark Shadows: A Report on the Lives and Struggles of Workers in Bhilai* (Delhi: PUDR, June 1991).
50. Sudip Chaudhuri, *Indigenous Firms in Relation to Transnational Corporations in the Drug Industry in India*, Ph.D. thesis, Jawaharlal Nehru University (New Delhi: Jawaharlal Nehru University, 1984); and Chaudhuri, 'Dunkel Draft'.
51. Amiya K. Bagchi, 'Transnational Banks, US Power Game and Global Impoverishment', *Economic & Political Weekly*, vol. 27, no. 22 (May 30, 1992) pp. 1133–6.
52. S.K. Khanna, 'Deregulation and Competition in Indian Industry: Anatomy of Rent Seeking Behaviour in the Corporate Sector', paper presented at a seminar on New Economic Policy (Calcutta: Indian Institute of Management (IIM), August 19–21, 1993).
53. Karl Polanyi, *The Great Transformation: The Political and Economic Origins of Our Time* (Boston, MA: Beacon, 1944).
54. Daniel R. Fusfeld, 'The Market in History', *Monthly Review*, vol. 45/1 (May 1993) pp. 1–8.
55. Maria Szecsi, 'Looking Back on the Great Transformation', *Monthly Review*, vol. 30 (January 1979) pp. 34–45.

# 4 Impacts of Neoliberal Policies in Sri Lanka

*Tissa Balasuriya*, OMI

## INTRODUCTION

Since July 1977 a pro-capitalist and pro-Western government of Sri Lanka has been implementing measures associated with economic liberalization and structural adjustment. These policies have been implemented in consultation with and under pressure from the Bretton Woods institutions (BWIs) and foreign aid donor countries. The BWIs' structural adjustment programs (SAPs) changed Sri Lanka's economic policies and economic institutions to conform to orthodox neoclassical economics including *laissez-faire* and free trade. This set of policies is referred to as 'neoliberalism'.

In theory, neoliberal policies are intended to change the economic position of a country through rapid industrialization, transfer of technology and the availability of credit and foreign aid, such as loans, grants and investment. In practice, neoliberal policies go further. They affect the whole gamut of economic and social relations of a country with impacts on gender, race and ethnic relations. Through neoliberal policies countries are further integrated into the world economic system where the transnational corporations (TNCs) dominate many lines of production, distribution, research and technology. The local political authority is compelled to help the TNCs as a condition for further aid.

Theoretically, poor countries are supposed to gain from the introduction of new technology and skills, the transfer of some factories to poor countries, the provision of new lines of employment, the improvement in communication infrastructure. If a country is careful, not too dependent on the foreign sources and not involved in internal conflicts, it may develop to a newly industrialized country (NIC). However, few developing countries are independent from foreign sources and enjoying internal peace; nor is the model of industrialization widely replicable. Some countries have to pay the price for others to advance in this competitive, anti-social, ecologically harmful process. The power of TNCs grows with their mergers and the take-over of state and private enterprises. The local elites share economic benefits with the TNCs but not with the local poor, nor do any benefits lead to environmentally sustainable development.

The BWIs propose SAPs as a universal panacea for all countries and all situations, except of course, for the governments of industrialized countries which are themselves in debt. Many organizations like the United Nations International Children's Emergency Fund (UNICEF), the United Nations Development Programme (UNDP), the International Labor Organisation (ILO) and the UN Economic Commission for Africa (UNECA) have raised substantial and legitimate challenges about SAPs, especially in Africa.[1]

This chapter distinguishes between the expressed goals and the real effects of neoliberal policies, especially of SAPs and trade liberalizations. It distinguishes between the rhetoric and the reality in the case of Sri Lanka. It is now well-documented that poverty and income distribution worsened in Sri Lanka since 1977 although the BWIs dispute these facts.[2] The next section analyzes the deterioration of some aggregate macroeconomic variables. A sectoral analysis of the impacts of neoliberal policies and of recent multilateral trade agreements follows. The impacts on government activity, human rights, women and the environment are summarized before the last section concludes with remarks on the need for an informed national dialogue.

## DETERIORATION OF SOME MACROECONOMIC VARIABLES

SAPs and trade liberalizations are said to save foreign exchange. They have actually increased the foreign dependency of Sri Lanka due to several factors:

- Devaluations did not have the effect they were supposed to have. They were expected to increase exports and reduce imports. With the exception of 1987, the Sri Lankan rupee depreciated continuously in value against the US dollar from 8.86 Rs/US$ at the end of 1976 to 46.00 Rs/US$ at the end of 1992.[3] However, the trade balance worsened from Special Drawing Right (SDR) 6 million in 1976 to SDR 686 million in 1992.

- Trade liberalizations led to a considerable increase in imports which have not been matched by similar increases in exports. While imports increased more than four times compared to their 1976 level, exports increased less than three times compared to their 1976 level.[4]
- The terms of trade worsened. The terms-of-trade index decreased continuously from 103 in 1985, to 100 in 1987 to 90 in 1992. This meant that Sri Lanka has to export more and more to get the same amount of imports.

There is a correlation between the trade deficits and the need for foreign aid, grants and loans to finance the trade deficit. The need for help in financing the trade deficit is linked to the increase in external debt and the debt-service payments which are themselves linked to budget deficits, since most of the external debt and debt-service payments are those of the Sri Lankan government.

### *Budget Deficits*

Neoliberal policies are expected to increase government revenues and reduce government deficits. However, they often reduce the state's earning capacity by transferring profit-making public enterprises to foreigners and/or local private enterprises (for example, Sri Lanka State Distilleries Corporation and Ceylon Oxygen) at give-away prices. Foreign investors are permitted to repatriate 100 per cent of profits. There is often a loss of revenue due to tax concessions to the new owners, thereby making the burden of indirect taxes heavier on the poor.

In the case of Sri Lanka, central government revenues have not increased but have hovered around 20 per cent of GDP since the 1970s.[5] Although overall government expenditures increased in the first few years of the pro-capitalist government, the government subsequently decreased social expenditures. The stagnation of government revenues and the initial increase in government expenditures have increased government deficits from 5.1 per cent of GDP (in 1972) to 18.4 per cent of GDP (in 1980). Further cuts in social expenditures reduced the deficit to 6.4 per cent of GDP in 1993.[6]

*Increasing Foreign Debt and Debt-Service Payments*

SAPs are expected to help the debtor countries to meet their debt obligations and to improve their financial situation. As Table 4.1 shows, Sri Lanka's external debt increased every year in terms of both rupees and SDRs. Sri Lanka's external debt increased also in terms of its ratio to GDP.[7] Since Sri Lanka's external debt will have to be repaid at some time, they represent a burden for future Sri Lankan generations. External debt-service payments increased every year in terms of rupees. There were a few years when the external debt-service payments decreased in terms of SDRs. This reflects the devaluation of the rupee but does not imply a decrease in the government's burden, since the Sri Lankan government raised its revenues mainly from domestic sources. Sri Lanka's interest-rate payments on its external debt averaged more than 100 million SDRs per year from 1985–91.[8]

At the global level, the stark reality is that at present there is no net aid or financial transfer from the rich to the poor countries. The cumulative net transfer on debt from poor countries to rich countries is more than $190 billion for 1985–91, averaging more than $27 billion per year.[9] Even if foreign loans are counted as aid, there is still a net transfer from poor to rich countries. In this perspective, the foreign aid received by the poor countries amounts to foreign assistance to repay foreign creditors. Excluding foreign investment, Sri Lanka was a net exporter of foreign currency in 1987 and in 1989, when it transferred net $16 million and $74 million respectively to the industrialized countries.

## IMPACTS ON MACROECONOMIC SECTORS

### *Agriculture*

The very forces which encourage global food production are also conducive to a contraction in the standard of living and decline in the local demand for food. Food aid from excess supplies in rich countries discourages local food production, changes food habits, encouraging consumption of foreign products and processed food often subsidized by governments in the European Community (EC) and North America.[10]

Table 4.1: External Debt and Debt-Service Payment

| Year | *External Debt* Rs. m. | SDR m. | *External Debt-Service Payment* Rs. m. | SDR m. |
|---|---|---|---|---|
| 1960 | 225 | n.a. | 33 | n.a. |
| 1970 | 1,550 | 419 | 623 | 76.2 |
| 1975 | 5,625 | 623 | 1,023 | 121.4 |
| 1976 | 6,826 | 666 | 1,074 | 110.3 |
| 1977 | 13,321 | 705 | 1,212 | 116.3 |
| 1978 | 17,276 | 854 | 2,347 | 119.8 |
| 1979 | 19,240 | 948 | 2,383 | 118.4 |
| 1980 | 25,828 | 1,203 | 2,763 | 137.0 |
| 1981 | 29,172 | 1,222 | 4,450 | 197.4 |
| 1982 | 34.597 | 1,506 | 5,217 | 227.5 |
| 1983 | 70,697 | 2,722 | 7,136 | 287.1 |
| 1984 | 80,839 | 3,126 | 8,026 | 308.0 |
| 1985 | 94,449 | 3,273 | 9,362 | 341.0 |
| 1986 | 117,093 | 3,378 | 12,376 | 370.2 |
| 1987 | 147,088 | 3,431 | 14,539 | 383.3 |
| 1988 | 162,548 | 3,679 | 17,207 | 402.8 |
| 1989 | 204,012 | 3,939 | 17,138 | 374.7 |
| 1990 | 233,971 | 4,121 | 17,971 | 328.5 |
| 1991 | 276,069 | 4,598 | 20,010 | 353.5 |
| 1992 | 313,279 | 5,029 | 23,478 | 372.7 |

Source: Central Bank of Sri Lanka: *Annual Report 1994*, Table 37 and Review of the Economy (Colombo: Central Bank of Sri Lanka, 1994).

Neoliberal policies foster the take-over of prime agricultural land by foreign TNCs for export crops. Resources are locked up for export purposes while people starve. Trade and foreign-exchange liberalizations replace foods crops with export crops thus increasing dependence on foreign markets, altogether a long-term 'recipe for starvation'. Agricultural extension services have been neglected in the process of reducing public expenditure. The agricultural marketing services of the state have also been reduced and the development of cooperatives neglected.

All of these measures have reduced the communication of

better production methods to farmers. The lack of agricultural planning and marketing services has sometimes led to farmers being unable to obtain reasonable prices at harvest times. Relative neglect of agricultural production and of the development of agro-industries, the reduction of subsidies on food and more recently the removal of the subsidy on fertilizers are making life hard for the poorer population, especially for farmers. Their frustration has led some farmers to commit suicide.

Sri Lanka's neoliberal policies have reduced food production, driven small farmers out of production and ownership of their lands, making them agricultural laborers, or increasing the urban unemployed. The sturdy peasantry is increasingly transformed into an army of landless seasonal plantation workers. On the other hand those who control the market exploit both the poor rural producer and the urban consumer.

Control of seed markets by the giant agro-industrial enterprises such as Cargill Inc. establishing 'plant breeder rights' leads to further impoverishment of millions of small farmers and to the destruction of biodiversity. Pesticides used in export agriculture damage the ecological equilibrium. Commercial land over-utilization contributes not only to environmental degradation but also to reduced agricultural productivity. Some of the state-owned tea, rubber and coconut plantations have been handed over to private (often foreign) management. These companies run down these valuable assets to earn quick returns during the years of their management contracts, which is then reported as increased productivity. Overall, there is a tendency to export what is produced and to import what is consumed, with deteriorating terms of trade.

There is considerable hypocrisy in the large industrialized countries. They recommend neoliberal agricultural policies to others while they maintain protectionist agricultural policies, keeping prices up and developing country goods out. While removing tariffs internally, the new trade blocs such as the European Union (EU) and the North American Free Trade Agreement (NAFTA) construct new forms of protectionism against those outside.[11]

Neoliberal policies change relations among nations. The poor countries return to colonial status through the controls exercised by the BWIs, which in turn are controlled by the rich powers: the United States, Western Europe and Japan, with the connivance of the benefiting local elites.

*Industry*

Neoliberal policies imply a false dichotomy between import substitution and export promotion. Contrary to neoliberal theory, some of the most spectacular successes of export-oriented growth came after a preparatory phase of intense import substitution with very strong state intervention as in South Korea.[12] Import substitution and export promotion can and generally need to be complementary. In addition, trade policies should be accompanied with an industrial strategy:

> The key lesson from the success of South Korea and Taiwan is that they did not rely solely on trade policies but combined trade policies with an industrial strategy to attain a high level of industrialization. Replication of the experience of these countries will not be easy given the initial conditions in Sri Lanka and the current global environment.[13]

Although neoliberal policies are said to be in favor of industrialization, in Sri Lanka several incipient industries had to close down after the 1977 liberalization. Thousands of handlooms and many small industries producing basic items, like matches, soap, salt, treacle and copra, which were once popular cottage industries, gradually declined in production. Some were eliminated from the market due to import liberalization. As a result, there is increased poverty, unemployment, regional disparities and a growing external dependence.

While Sri Lanka's garment industry has expanded rapidly since 1989, it is seriously threatened by the adoption of the rules of the World Trade Organization (WTO) and by improved technology in industrialized countries. The adoption of regional trade agreements like NAFTA implies another threat to Sri Lanka's textile exports to North America. Other negative characteristics of the garment industry include:

- profits produced by cheap exploited labor go largely to foreign owners of modernized factories;

- increasing dependence on a competitive, volatile international market, and

- increased imports of intermediate inputs, which means there is little value added within Sri Lanka.

Trade liberalizations encourage luxury imports while the poor cannot afford basic needs. Neoliberal policies discourage adequate long-term planning of industrial growth. Liberalizations do not safeguard the national ownership of enterprises. Raw materials are practically given away for industrial processing elsewhere; there is virtually no transfer of technology or know-how. Technology transfers will be even less likely in the future given the increased protection for the intellectual property rights of foreign capital owners through the WTO agreements.

*Services*

There is a well-documented difference in the structure of the economy between more and less developed countries: the more developed a country, the higher is the percentage of the service sector as a portion of GDP. This structural difference provides the more developed countries with a comparative advantage in the service sector, based on more modern technology and know-how. Within the process of development, it is expected that the service sector will be the sector which grows the most.

Based on this fact, industrialized countries have successfully pushed the inclusion of trade in services and the international protection of property rights into the multilateral trade negotiations. Protecting developing-country service-sector industries from the more advanced service sectors of industrialized countries will be difficult under the new multilateral trade agreements, especially the General Agreement on Trade in Services (GATS). Adopting and imitating new technology, one of the main aspects of Japan's development, is basically ruled out through the Agreement on Trade-Related Aspects of Intellectual Property Rights (TRIPS). If developing countries want to use the more efficient technologies, most of which have been developed in the industrialized countries, either they will not be allowed to use them at all or they will have to pay considerable royalties. Thus, industrialized countries have successfully blocked a free flow of knowledge within the world. This will constitute an added barrier for the developing countries to become developed countries. The other alternative is that developing countries develop their service sectors but the benefits will go to the owners of the most efficient technologies in the already rich countries.

## SOME OTHER ASPECTS OF NEOLIBERAL POLICIES

### *Reduction of State Activity*

Neoliberal policies advocate reduced state activity in the economic field as a condition for economic growth. They therefore demand the privatization of all state-owned economic enterprises and the deregulation of the private sector. But the reality is that the nations that have advanced economically like Japan and the East Asian newly industrialized countries have had strong governments directing the economy. They fostered and protected their enterprises against foreign competition, at least until they were strong enough to compete successfully with others. They also created the environment for economic growth by subsidizing credit and by carrying out land reforms, thereby increasing local food production. Their opening to the free market was in an orderly and calculated manner, following success; in contrast, Sri Lanka's opening is injudicious and from a position of weakness.

The policy of privatization is being pushed relentlessly by the BWIs. Once again the main industrial, agricultural and service sectors of the aid-dependent poor countries are falling into the hands of the local elites and the big TNCs. Privatization of state-owned enterprises increases the prices of services for the poor – electricity, water and irrigation, roads and transportation; while it tends to subsidize private investors. Deregulation of private enterprise leaves room for much corruption and favoritism even in the process of privatization.

The BWIs' neoliberal policies demobilize the state in poor countries, and rely on the mercy of market forces. Since the domestic private sector is weak in most developing countries the removal of the state's countervailing power renders the country defenseless against the powerful TNCs. On the contrary, in the rich countries the state exercises a strong regulatory function on the economy.[14]

With the introduction of neoliberal policies, countries increase their dependency on foreign aid in order to balance the budget. The governments agree to donors' conditions in order to survive. The sovereignty of poor countries is thus undermined by the conditionalities placed on aid. Their budget and policy decisions are made at Paris-based Consultative Group meetings of donors.

*Social and Human Rights Concerns*

The rich countries express concern over human rights, and rightly so; yet SAPs deny human rights in social and economic spheres. Neoliberal policies and the introduction of free trade are hard on the poor by reducing subsidies, cutting social services, requiring fees for education and health services and increasing relative prices paid by the poor.[15] Wages are kept low, inequalities increase and the social services built up in the previous era are reduced if not abolished. Strikes are effectively banned, job security reduced and labor laws tightened against workers.

The neoliberal approach has increased social inequality and widened the gap between the rich and the poor. Cost of living increased and, in some cases, famines have resulted:[16]

> The social disasters produced by the SAP are not the result of marginal errors which can be corrected by so called 'structural adjustment with a human face', or 'integrating the social dimension in the programmes' etc. They are the logical and necessary consequences of what is wanted.[17]

Despite the rhetoric of democracy, there is a lack of transparency in discussions and decisions regarding conditionalities imposed on the debtor countries. Such conditions are not subject to parliamentary debate, nor are they ever shared with select parliamentary committees, much less with the general public affected by them. If this trend continues, political violence may erupt as the only language that the corrupt and powerful recognize.

The worsening social conditions have led to increased social discontent and violence, increase in expenditure for defense, prisons, law and order. As the country becomes poorer and there is less of a surplus for the ruling classes, there is a tendency for them to resort to other forms of manipulation of the people. Ethnicism is one such approach. These are partly the causes of Sri Lanka's ethnic conflict. The fact that the eruption of ethnic conflict in Sri Lanka coincided with the liberalization of the economy and the strengthening of SAPs leaves room for questioning whether the civil war is not partly the result of neoliberal policies. The worsening social conditions have meant that the government has ruled using emergency regulations for nearly two decades. There are now new measures for tightening these emergency laws to prevent public criticism of the Sri Lankan government and its policies.

*Exploitation of Women*

Free trade and SAPs have meant the greater exploitation of women in many aspects:

- Women's rights are not safeguarded but sacrificed for the sake of earning foreign exchange.
- Young women are exploited in free trade zones without workers' associations and without suitable conditions of work or living.
- Women are compelled to migrate to foreign countries to earn foreign exchange to make ends meet due to increase in prices and unemployment of males.
- Families break up with serious consequences on social and moral life, neglect of children and an increase in prostitution including child prostitution.
- High prices, food shortages and worsening conditions of health place heavier burdens on the women in terms of more time in food preparation and in the care of sick family members.

For a more detailed analysis of the negative impacts of neoliberal policies on the women of Sri Lanka see the contribution by Swarna Jayaweera.[18]

*Ecological Damage*

The reduction of the productive capacity of Sri Lanka has been hidden in the statistics by running down non-renewable resources such as forests, minerals, gems and coastline fisheries, since depletions of these resources count as increases in standard national income accounting. In 1945 the forest cover was estimated at 45 per cent of Sri Lanka; now it is estimated at about 20 per cent despite some government efforts at reforestation. However, every tree cut still continues to increase GDP. TNCs are largely not accountable for the damage they cause.

## CONCLUSION: THE NEED FOR AN INFORMED NATIONAL DIALOGUE

All the above indicates that it is time to examine more carefully the ideological claims of neoliberal policies and free trade. An intellectual neocolonialism tends to accept the free trade paradigm rather uncritically. The poor countries need to regain their capacity to design their own future after careful investigation of the results of the past two decades. An informed national dialogue is essential; people most affected by these policies must have a voice in deciding their future.

It is to be feared that instead of developing into a Singapore, Taiwan or South Korea, Sri Lanka is on a disastrous trend towards situations like those in Somalia or Bosnia with their social and ethnic civil conflicts. Facing these issues with full consciousness of their import and gravity is one of the main spiritual challenges for Sri Lanka with its long spiritual and cultural heritage that it should not fritter away for the mess of pottage offered as foreign loans. The resistance to these measures may grow as the poverty of the masses increases and as the poor in the rich countries also feel the pinch of the marginalization by the powerful.

There are certain imperatives in the present economic situation of poor countries which have to be recognized and dealt with, with or without the BWIs' recommendations. A country must learn to live within its means. Budget deficits and balance-of-payments deficits must be reduced. Losses and waste in the public sector must be avoided. Bribery, corruption and favoritism must be eliminated. Civil wars must be ended with peace and justice to all. There must be freedom for enterprise and reward for work and initiative. Free trade is not necessarily bad, but if industrialized and developing countries fight over markets the developing countries will lose.

There must be a return to the accent on the social function of the economy and of the state. But for many poor who will be eliminated during the coming decade, this will be too late. Despite all the technological advancement, the 1990s may be a most cruel decade. Humanity's hope is in the rise of a social and moral consciousness that leads to a global peoples' movement for the transformation of persons and structures at local, national and global levels.

## NOTES

1. See the annual reports of United Nations International Children's Emergency Fund (UNICEF), *State of the World's Children* (Oxford and New York: Oxford University Press for UNICEF); United Nations Development Programme (UNDP), *Human Development Report* (New York: Oxford University Press, various issues); and United Nations Economic Commission for Africa (UNECA), *African Alternative Framework to Structural Adjustment Programme for Socio-Economic Recovery and Transformation* (Addis Ababa: UNECA, 1989).
2. See, for example, Nanak Kakwani, *Income Inequality, Welfare and Poverty in a Developing Economy with Applications to Sri Lanka*, Wider Working Papers, WP 4 (Helsinki: World Institute for Development Economics Research; and Tokyo: United Nations University, April 1986) p. 30; Martin Ravallion and Sisira Jayasuriya, 'Liberalization and Inequality in Sri Lanka: A Comment', *Journal of Development Economics*, vol. 28 (March 1988) pp. 247–55; and Sarath Divisekera, and B.S. Felmingham, 'Sri Lankan Economic Performance and Income Distribution in Various Policy Epochs', *The Singapore Economic Review*, vol. 34/1 (April 1989) pp. 43–9.

   According to a survey by the Central Bank of Sri Lanka, 60 per cent of Sri Lankans receive only 25 per cent of the national income, while the wealthier 40 per cent receive 75 per cent. The survey also reveals that the poorest 10 per cent have become even poorer since the previous survey in 1981–82 (as cited in the Economic Intelligence Unit's *Country Report (on Sri Lanka)*, 4th Quarter, 1994 p. 13).
3. See Central Bank of Sri Lanka, *Bulletin* of September 1993, Tables 33 and 34; and International Monetary Fund (IMF), *International Financial Statistics*, vol. 47/7 (Washington, DC: IMF, July 1994) for details.
4. See for example, Central Bank of Sri Lanka, *Annual Report 1992*, Table 1.39 (Colombo: Central Bank of Sri Lanka, 1992) p. 92.
5. See various issues of World Bank, *World Development Report* (New York: Oxford University Press), Table 12: 'Central Government Current Revenue'.
6. See various issues of World Bank, *World Development Report* (New York: Oxford University Press), Table 11: 'Central Government Expenditure'.
7. In terms of external debt to GDP, the ratio increased from less than 50 per cent in 1980 to over 75 per cent in 1991. See various issues

of World Bank, *World Development Report* (New York: Oxford University Press), Table 23: 'Total external debt ratios'.

8. World Bank, *World Debt Tables 1992–93*, vol. II (Washington, DC: World Bank, 1992) p. 372.
9. World Bank, *World Debt Tables 1992–93*, vol. I (Washington, DC: World Bank, 1992) p. 160.
10. This became most clear in West Africa, where subsidized beef and dairy products imported (duty-free) from the European Community (EC) have led to the demise of Africa's nomadic pastoral economy. European beef imports to West Africa increased seven-fold since 1984: 'Low quality EC beef sells at half the price of locally produced meat. Swahilian farmers are finding out that no-one is prepared to buy their herds.' See Leslie Crawford, 'West Africans Hurt by EC Beef Policy', *Financial Times*, May 21, 1993.
11. Japan, an important shareholder in the BWIs and in the Asian Development Bank (ADB) is protectionist even against US exports.
12. See Dani Rodrik, *Getting Interventions Right: How South Korea and Taiwan Grew Rich*, Working Paper No. 4964 (Cambridge: National Bureau of Economic Research, December 1994); and Lal Jayawardena, 'Market-Friendly Policies: An Appraisal', *MARGA (Sri Lanka Centre for Development Studies) Quarterly Journal*, vol. 13/2 (1994) pp. 1–18.
13. Saman Kelegama and Ganeshan Wignaraja 'Trade Policy and Industrial Development in Sri Lanka', *MARGA (Sri Lanka Centre for Development Studies) Quarterly Journal*, vol. 11/4 (1991) p. 49.
14. For example, the Canadian Wheat Marketing Board controls agricultural production and marketing of the Canadian wheat market.
15. The effects of relative prices of Sri Lanka's recent structural adjustment program on the poorest segments of society are analyzed in Anne-Marie Gulde, 'Sri Lanka: Price Changes and the Poor', *IMF Working Paper*, WP/91/46 (Washington, DC: IMF, May 1991).
16. Poverty in Sri Lanka became so bad that the late President Premadas in 1988 proposed a vote-catching Poverty Alleviation Programme, called *Janasaviya*, of giving income subsidies and a capital of Rs. 25,000 to the poorer families to help them overcome their poverty.
17. Seamer Amin, Keynote Address to a Workshop 'Beyond Structural Adjustment', Partnership Africa-Canada, Ottawa, September 27–29, 1993, referring to G.A. Cornia, R. Jolly and F. Stewart (eds), *Adjustment with a Human Face – Protecting the Vulnerable and Promoting Growth*, vols I and II, A UNICEF Study (Oxford: Clarendon Press, 1987).
18. Swarna Jayaweera, 'Structural Adjustment Policies, Industrial Development and Women in Sri Lanka' in Pamela Sparr (ed.), *Mortgaging Women's Lives: Feminist Critiques of Structural Adjustment* (London and New Jersey: Zed Books, 1994) pp. 96–115.

# 5 Rethinking Corporate Accountability

*John Cavanagh*

## HOW TO THINK ABOUT CORPORATE ACCOUNTABILITY

### *The Problem*

Two hundred giant corporations, most of them larger than many economies, now control over a quarter of the world's economic activity.[1] For example, Philip Morris is larger than New Zealand, and it operates in 170 countries.[2] Instead of creating an integrated global village, these firms are weaving webs of production, consumption and finance that bring economic benefits to, at most, a third of the world's people. Two-thirds of the world (the bottom 20 per cent of the rich countries and the bottom 80 per cent of the poor countries) are either left out, marginalized, or hurt by these webs of activity.

Over the past century, as corporations and banks have shifted from local operations to regional, then national, and now global terrains, they have severed ties with local communities and workers with whom they once had a close and symbiotic bond. As corporations compete in a brutal global economy which includes segments of every country, their top executives seldom express concerns for the social and environmental impact of their policies on communities or even nations. Executives will often point out that it is not in their domain to worry about job loss in France or the trade deficit in the United States. Their concern is to minimize costs by picking from a global menu of options where to produce, sell, finance and trade.

In a world where the most dynamic economic actors are global and yet governments remain local and national, deep problems emerge. In particular, governments attempt to grapple with community welfare, jobs and the environment at a time when their largest corporations are slashing jobs, abandoning communities and competing globally by shaving environmental and labor costs. In the name of competing globally, corporations are now contributing to the most pressing global job and environmental crises the planet has ever faced.

*Lack of Corporate Accountability*

Corporations profess accountability to shareholders, yet in an age where their shares are traded on stock exchanges around the world, it is increasingly difficult to get a grip on who those shareholders are. Mutual funds, pension funds and other investors shift their portfolios continuously as they respond to around-the-clock market information. Corporate executives also often claim that their global extensions are serving consumers through greater variety and cheaper prices on goods made in countries where wages are kept low. Sometimes this is true, but in increasingly concentrated markets, firms seldom lower prices.[3]

Despite some accountability to faceless shareholders and consumers, corporate accountability to communities, to workers, to the environment, and to the countries in which they are chartered is on the decline. If Green Giant can get away with dumping toxic substances in Mexican soil in order to undercut its competitors for the US market, it will do so.[4] If the Ford Motor Company can reduce costs by flagrantly violating the rights of Mexican auto workers, it will do so.[5] If General Motors, AT&T, and IBM can compete better by announcing work-force reductions of over 70,000 each since 1991, they will do so.[6] If firms in richer countries can bargain down wages, working conditions and health and safety standards by threatening workers and governments that they will shift production elsewhere, they will do so.

This lack of corporate accountability is less pronounced in Japan, Korea, Taiwan and Germany where, historically, firms have had close bonds with government to advance national economic and security goals. Yet even in these countries the bonds are weakening in the face of global competition.

Corporations have also hijacked the agendas of intergovernmental bodies and twisted these institutions to serve their narrow corporate needs rather than larger social goals. Thus, private banks turned the International Monetary Fund (IMF) into their own collection agency after the emergence of a global debt crisis in 1982.[7] Agrichemical and agribusiness firms have used the World Bank as a global market opener. The Uruguay Round of the General Agreement on Tariffs and Trade (GATT) established the World Trade Organization (WTO) and provided the investment and intellectual property protections that many firms had been seeking in order to operate more profitably globally. Hence, as urgent as the task to rethink the Bretton Woods institutions is the task of creating new mechanisms to promote corporate accountability.

### *Countervailing Power*

On the surface, it appears as though countervailing power against global corporations is weak. Unions are on the decline in almost every country. Governments, instead of placing more responsibilities on corporations, have been offering them greater global mobility and rights through deregulating agreements like the North American Free Trade Agreement (NAFTA) and the agreements of WTO.

The momentum behind this deregulatory agenda, however, is on the wane. A corporate accountability movement that grew rapidly in the 1970s was partly destroyed by the free-market triumphalism of the Reagan, Bush, Thatcher, and Kohl administrations. The collapse of socialist regimes in Eastern Europe in the late 1980s reinforced the momentum. By the mid-1990s, however, the problems of a privatized and deregulated global market economy are becoming evident everywhere.

In many parts of the world, people's organizations are fighting corporate abuses against communities, workers and the environment. In the fight over NAFTA, a broad array of citizen movements from Mexico, the United States, and Canada fought an agreement that steered the benefits of integration to a few thousand large corporations often at the expense of large segments of society. Unions have formed innovative alliances to organize across borders. Religious groups have been at the forefront of using shareholder resolutions to press corporate responsibility. Environmental groups such as Greenpeace have targeted large firms that have spread unsafe production facilities and toxic wastes around the world. Increasingly, these movements are recognizing that they have many tools at their disposal with which to address the lack of corporate accountability.

Many of these fights have simply been at the level of survival: communities and workers clashing with corporations over the pollution of water or air, or over corporate decisions to shut down plants, or over corporate abuses of workers' basic rights. In recent decades, however, two arenas where citizen groups have attempted to increase their power over corporate abuses have been attempts to amend trade agreements and the establishment of codes of conduct. Each of these two arenas is examined in turn.

## CORPORATE ACCOUNTABILITY THROUGH TRADE AGREEMENTS

A portion of the corporate accountability problems that communities now face was foreseen by the architects of the post-war global economic institutions. The original Havana Charter for an International Trade Organization (ITO) included a proposal for an international antitrust law.[8] It contained a chapter on 'Restrictive Business Practices' of transnational corporations (TNCs). It included measures to address employment and worker rights. The US business community attacked these proposals and the US Congress never ratified the ITO. Instead, the much more restricted GATT was set up which dealt quite narrowly with the issue of reducing tariff barriers to trade and failed to address the larger social problems.

Hence, part of today's agenda around corporate accountability was debated 50 years ago. Many argued that GATT should have a 'social clause' which defined the violation of workers' basic rights as unfair trade practices punishable by trade sanctions. As the broader International Trade Organization was never ratified, so too was this defeated.

### *US Trade Law and Worker Rights*

As early as the late nineteenth century, workers and worker rights advocates have fought successfully to link respect for worker rights to trade benefits. The McKinley Tariff Act of 1890 prohibited the domestic trade of goods made by convicts in the United States.[9] Over the ensuing decades, there were a number of related measures that limited US imports of goods made by prison labor. The movement to link trade to worker rights, however, really took off in the United States in the 1980s when labor, human rights and religious activists created the International Labor Rights Education and Research Fund. The participating groups studied 70 years of International Labor Organisation (ILO) deliberations in order to specify the most basic of internationally-recognized worker rights: freedom of association, the right to collective bargaining, bans on child and prison labor and minimum standards with respect to wages, working conditions and health and safety standards.

Working with allies in the US Congress, these groups helped to craft US legislation to link US trade and investment privileges to other countries' respect for basic worker rights. The US corporate community, viewing the legislation as an infringement on their freedom to exploit differences in the respect for rights in different countries, fought the linkage. Yet on four occasions over the past decade, the US Congress has passed legislation linking trade and investment privileges to respect for worker rights. First, in 1984, the US Generalized System of Preferences whereby many goods from the Third World entered the United States without paying tariffs was amended so that if a country was found to be violating internationally-recognized worker rights, it could be denied the duty-free benefits. Similar amendments were attached to the Overseas Private Investment Corporation, the Caribbean Basin Initiative, and the Trade Act of 1988.

Threats by the US government to withdraw trade preferences have led to important reforms in a number of countries. For instance, in response to looming US sanctions, El Salvador worked with the ILO to adopt a more comprehensive labor code. The government of Sri Lanka reacted to similar pressure by agreeing to open its garment industry to collective bargaining. Indonesia announced a 29 per cent increase in its minimum wage in 1994 after the United States threatened to remove trade preferences.

### *NAFTA and Western Hemisphere*

When a free-trade area for North America was first proposed by US President George Bush and Mexican President Carlos Salinas in 1990, broad citizen movements formed to fight the agreement and to propose alternative integration agreements that would impose responsibilities on global firms to balance the new global rights they would receive under NAFTA.

In the end, pressure from these groups led the US government to propose the negotiation of side agreements to NAFTA on the environment and on labor. Hundreds of TNCs banded together in a corporate alliance (for example, USA*NAFTA) which opposed the side agreements and, in the final agreement, the linkage between trade and labor and environmental rights was quite weak.

The Clinton administration continues to pursue a strategy of extending free trade to the entire Western Hemisphere piece by piece. The next areas that are slated to be folded into agreements on the NAFTA model are Chile and the Caribbean Basin. Citizen groups from the hemisphere have seized upon this agenda to argue that NAFTA should not be the model for hemispheric integration, but rather that new provisions to advance worker and environmental rights and standards should be at the core of new agreements.

### *GATT/WTO*

Over the past decade, there has also been a concerted attempt by trade unions, other groups and some governments to amend the GATT to include worker rights and, more recently, environmental rights and standards. This strategy has proved among the most controversial even among various citizen groups.

Despite widespread support for this linkage among trade unions in North and South,[10] the Third World Network in Malaysia has rallied a number of Southern citizen groups against the linkage on a number of grounds. In a paper by Martin Khor (1994), the Network charges that the attempt to place labor standards in the World Trade Organization (WTO) 'is quite clearly prompted not by feelings of goodwill towards Third World workers, but by protectionist attempts to prevent the transfer of jobs from the North to the South'.[11] While different supporters of the workers rights linkage have different motivations, this statement is false. When the Scandinavian unions and governments pressed for a social charter in GATT over the years, their motivation was the improvement of worker rights in the developing world. When the United States started to push for the linkage in 1984, it was the result of the pressure of labor rights advocates from unions, churches, and human rights groups working with independent trade unions in Chile, the Philippines, Indonesia, Guatemala, Haiti and elsewhere. These groups lobbied the US Congress to include worker rights in the GATT, and the US Congress pressed this agenda on the administration. The overall motivation of these groups includes a desire to reduce the power of US firms to bargain down US wages and conditions by threatening to move offshore; the motivation is not protectionist.

The Third World Network is also worried that placing labor rights in trade agreements opens the door to declaring a series of other issues as 'trade-related' and using them in a protectionist manner. Yet, the evidence is quite strong that worker rights are definitely trade-related. TNCs routinely use the violation of worker rights to gain unfair advantage in trade. The fact that the Ford Motor Company can achieve the same levels of productivity in Mexico as in the United States yet pay one-tenth the wages (because Mexican worker rights are denied) creates horrendously unfair trade advantages for Ford in Mexico. If this disparity is not addressed, Ford and other TNCs will bargain US worker rights and wages down to the least common denominator.

The Network also points out that the new WTO is Northern-dominated, secretive and undemocratic, and they argue that worker rights should be dealt with in the ILO. There is merit in this suggestion; the only problem is that the ILO lacks enforcement powers. Hence, trade unions favor a mechanism whereby it is still the ILO that determines worker rights conventions and the ILO would handle petitions on violations, yet it would be the trade agreements that have the enforcement powers of sanctions or fines. And, most groups pressing for labor and environmental rights in the WTO condition these changes on the organization becoming more democratic, more open to citizen groups, and more transparent.

There is a possible compromise position that emanates from a three-year discussion among Mexican, US and Canadian groups that concluded in a document entitled 'A Just and Sustainable Trade and Development Initiative for North America' (a document which is now being expanded to include inputs from the rest of the hemisphere).[12]

That document proposed an agreement that violations of internationally recognized labor and environmental rights and standards should be considered unfair trade practices in an alternative integration agreement, provided that:

- the dispute resolution mechanism be open to citizen input, be democratic, and Mexican or Canadian groups could challenge violations in the United States just as US groups could challenge violations in Mexico;

- the sanction for violation be centered on the violator, for example, the *corporation* violating labor or environmental rights through fines, and

- a number of measures be included in the overall agreement to reduce the inequalities between Mexico and the United States since the raising of labor and environmental standards in Mexico could discourage some new investment. These measures would include debt reduction, fundamental reform of the World Bank and IMF, and creation of new decentralized and democratic aid mechanisms that reach the poorer majority.

As these debates spread, labor and environmental issues are likely to dominate the next round of regional and world trade talks. Trade agreements are only one realm through which to advance these rights and standards. Equally important is the realm of government policy and corporate codes of conduct.

## CORPORATE CODES AND RELATED INITIATIVES

While trade agreements remain an important domain for the fight to advance corporate accountability, it is an imperfect one. The weapon of trade sanctions is a blunt one, often punishing the innocent with the guilty. If Paraguay is denied trade benefits because a number of firms in that country violate worker rights, many Paraguayans stand to suffer. Even if trade sanctions single out a specific industrial sector for punishment, the 'innocent' can suffer.

Hence, many citizen groups and governments have sought to create instruments that specifically target global corporations. Over the past couple of decades, thousands of different attempts have been launched, some even by corporations themselves. These fall into three broad categories: those by corporations, those by governments and those by citizen movements. Each is examined in turn in its various manifestations.

### *Codes by Corporations*

#### *Voluntary Codes by Corporate Associations*

Beginning in the 1970s, in an attempt to head off what they saw as more dangerous and potentially compulsory government codes, a number of corporate associations began to draw up their own voluntary codes of conduct. Some of these were sponsored by global groups such as the International Chamber of Commerce; others were advanced by firms in specific sectors, such as the

Pharmaceutical Manufacturers Association. All these efforts share the distinction that the principles and business practices that they seek to advance are voluntary.

One of the most recent efforts emerged from a group entitled the Caux Round Table, formed in 1986 by business leaders from Japan, Europe and the United States. Their 'Principles for Business' state that global corporations 'should play an important role in improving economic and social conditions' and they offer a series of principles for corporate activity toward consumers, employees, investors, suppliers, competitors and communities. Yet drafters of the Principles included executives from leading polluter 3M Company, rainforest destroyer Mitsubishi and other violators of labor and environmental rights.

*Individual Codes on Subcontractors*

Since the early 1990s, unions and human rights groups have focused public attention on one of the more dangerous trends in the globalization of production by large firms. As technological innovations have increased the ease with which firms can shift production to different sites, many firms began to subcontract parts of the production process to different countries. A Nike sneaker, for example, may have an air pocket manufactured in the United States, but it most likely has been assembled by a young woman in Indonesia or China. The factory in which the women work may be owned by Koreans or Indonesians or Chinese, but it isn't owned by Nike. As flagrant abuses of workers in such subcontractors began to reach the attention of human rights activists in the late 1980s, firms often responded by denying knowledge or responsibility for what happened in someone else's firm.

Increased pressure in the 1990s by human and labor rights groups led some firms to adopt their own voluntary codes of conduct for their subcontractors.[13] Sears and Levi Strauss, for example, agreed not to contract production to firms that used prison labor or committed other specified violations of worker rights. Persistent violations in China have prompted Levi Strauss to announce that they will phase out all production contracts in that country. Overall, Levi Strauss claims to have disconnected contracts with 35 of their roughly 700 subcontractors because of violations of their code.[14]

When President Clinton announced on May 26, 1994 that he was delinking human rights considerations from US trade policy to China, he did urge all US firms operating in China to adopt voluntary codes of standards to govern their operations there and the operations of their subcontractors. This offers an excellent opportunity for citizen groups to put forward a model code of conduct which could be put forward for all firms operating in China (and, by extension, to all transnational corporations).

*Codes by Governments*

Codes written by corporations have suffered both in weak content and poor monitoring and enforcement. This has led many in government and citizen movements to strive for more binding codes at the governmental and intergovernmental level.

*The United Nations and Other Intergovernmental Codes*

In the wake of the revelations around the role of AT&T in the Chilean coup of 1973, a strong movement for greater corporate accountability emerged around the world. With Third World governments raising a powerful call, the United Nations created a Commission on Transnational Corporations in 1975 which set out to negotiate a UN Code of Conduct on Transnational Corporations. The draft UN code prohibited bribery of public officials, required corporate disclosure of potential dangers of products and production processes, banned the export of goods or factories that were deemed unsafe in one country and a number of other measures. The Reagan administration strongly opposed the effort, and the negotiations collapsed. Yet a delineation of corporate responsibility in the global marketplace is now more urgent than ever. Without some clear international rules applicable to all global corporations, individual companies will continue to cut costs by shedding obligations to treat workers decently and to protect the environment.

Citizen groups such as the International Organization of Consumer Unions (IOCU) are working hard to revive interest in the UN Code of Conduct on Transnational Corporations or a similar set of guidelines and mechanisms on foreign direct investment. A number of groups that met in a Conference on Fairplay in Global Business, in Delhi, India, in February 1994, likewise committed themselves to this task.

Another UN body which has passed a code on corporate behavior is the International Labor Organisation (ILO). In 1977, the ILO adopted a 'Tripartite Declaration of Principles concerning Multinational Enterprises and Social Policy' which offers guidelines to governments, firms and workers in the areas of industrial relations, employment, training and working conditions. Likewise, in 1976, the developed country members of the United Nations used the Organization for Economic Cooperation and Development (OECD) to pass guidelines on 'International Investment and Multinational Enterprises' that encompass many of these same areas.

In addition to these omnibus codes, there have been instances when the United Nations has passed codes in specific areas. The most celebrated was the code on the marketing of infant formula jointly negotiated by the World Health Organization (WHO) and the United Nations International Children's Emergency Fund (UNICEF). The code prohibits transnational corporate infant formula producers from using deceptive marketing practices when selling baby food in developing countries. There have been movements to extend such marketing codes to pharmaceuticals, cigarettes and alcohol as well.

Environmental groups spearheaded by Greenpeace launched a major campaign in the 1990s to convince governments to place restrictions against the international trade in hazardous waste products. This campaign culminated in governments passing the Basle Convention on International Waste Trade.

Law professors Diane Orentlicher and Timothy Gelatt suggest that the Group of Seven (G-7) would be a good forum for a concerted effort at adherence to a set of global principles on transnational corporations.[15] Since the overwhelming majority of the world's TNCs originate in these seven countries, this might prove an easier arena than the United Nations.

One of the key issues for any code, be it global, among the industrial countries, or national, is enforcement. Corporations' familiar cry that codes be voluntary, to leave it to corporations to police themselves, is to invite non-compliance. Governments have it within their power to offer incentives for compliance without actually making codes compulsory.

Most governments offer incentives for firms to invest overseas. In the case of the United States, the Overseas Private Investment Corporation offers firms insurance on overseas investment. A foreign tax credit allows US firms to avoid paying US taxes on their foreign subsidiaries' activities if the subsidiaries are paying taxes in the host country. Portions of the tariff code offer incentives for firms to set up factories overseas to process US-made parts and send them back to the United States. All of these programs could be conditioned upon corporate compliance with a code of conduct based on the provisions of the UN code or the OECD code. The code would be 'voluntary' in the sense that firms could ignore it with impunity; yet if they wanted the benefit of the government programs, they would have to abide by the code.

*National Governments*

Most national governments have bought into the ideology of the global corporation, that government policy should be steered toward enhancing the competitiveness of the country and its firms. Unfortunately, this has often led to policies that encourage cost-cutting measures by firms, be it through cutting jobs, wages, or working standards. Governments must be pressed to reassert their more traditional goals of guaranteeing the welfare of those left out by the market, and helping to stimulate good jobs. There are a number of areas where governments have exerted positive pressure to steer corporate activity toward the common good of society. Eric Kolodner, in a study for the UN World Summit on Social Development, listed several, including:

> Corporate transparency through disclosure of information requirements, production processes through local content regulations, workplace conditions through labour legislation, and employment levels through mandated hiring of nationals. Governments have also enacted a host of financially oriented measures regulating banks, stock markets, divestment and the repatriation of profits. Additionally, governments have implemented legislation mandating local equity participation, property ownership limitations, transfer of technology requirements as well as responsible environmental and energy practices. Finally, governments have required transnational corporations to assist with macroeconomic issues through balance-of-payments clauses, anti-trust laws and import-export limitations.[16]

Unfortunately, most government action is not in this direction, but in the direction of loosening state restrictions on corporate activity. A change of heart back toward more active involvement in steering corporate activity toward social ends will only come through concerted citizen pressure.

*State/Provincial Governments*

Environmental activists Richard Grossman and Frank Adams remind us about the fundamental source of power over corporations. Corporations exist through charters that are granted by state governments. Originally, charters obligated firms to serve the common good; if they did not, the charter could be and sometimes was revoked.[17] By the late nineteenth century, corporations managed to subvert this original purpose; Grossman and Adams suggest that the time has come for citizens to get involved again in the chartering business. State governments could be encouraged to adopt a code of conduct that would accompany new charters. If companies violate the code, the charter would be revoked. Some activists in the United States are now considering a campaign to un-charter Union Carbide[18] on these grounds.

*Local Governments*

A similar idea has been advanced by Michael Shuman of the Institute for Policy Studies: the establishment of a code of practices among local government officials that spell out guidelines for corporate behavior.[19] This would prevent the kind of destructive playing-off of communities against one another that large corporations engage in as they seek the most attractive sites for new investments.

In a similar effort, the Council of Canadians is attempting to curb the destructive effect that the spread of Walmart is having on Canadian communities. They have assembled a list of demands that they are encouraging local officials to place on Walmart in exchange for the right to build new stores.

### *Codes and Initiatives by Citizen Movements*

It will be citizen movements creating pressure on governments and directly on corporations that will be central in the creation of codes and other mechanisms to promote corporate accountability. There is a rich history of such citizen involvement in many countries, originating primarily in unions, religious groups, farm groups, environmental organizations, consumer groups and women's organizations.

*Past Attempts*

There have been a number of successful examples of broad-based international citizen campaigns over the past two decades that have forced changes in corporate behavior and/or created new international mechanisms to help hold corporate power in check. Many of these were launched in the 1970s during the period of heightened global concern about the abuses of TNCs in the Third World. During much of the 1970s and 1980s. Northern and Southern religious and consumer groups collaborated to attack Nestle and other infant formula companies for deceptive marketing practices which induced mothers to forgo breastfeeding their children in favor of commercially-produced infant formula. Since water-borne disease is one of the primary killers in the developing world, powdered milk mixed with untreated water likewise transmits disease. Moreover, many poor families could ill-afford to spend their meager financial resources on a product that was available for free from breastfeeding mothers. These campaigns used the pressure of consumer boycotts which culminated in the World Health Organization/UNICEF marketing code.

An equally impressive campaign was launched in many countries involving state and municipal officials, unions, religious groups and others to pressure corporations to stop doing business in South Africa as a protest against the racist policy of apartheid. Participants used the pressures of selective investment, the power of government procurement contracts, divestment and other measures to help pressure the apartheid regime to free Nelson Mandela from prison and to hold the country's first universal elections.

Similar campaigns have been launched against hundreds of firms in recent decades using the power of individuals as consumers, workers, shareholders and depositors. A recent issue of *Co-op America Quarterly's* 'Boycott Action News' documented citizen campaigns against Philip Morris and 57 other companies by citizen groups around the country.[20]

*Shareholder Resolutions*

The Interfaith Center for Corporate Responsibility (ICCR) is a 23-year-old association of nearly 250 religious organizations. Over the past year, ICCR members have submitted 198 shareholder resolutions to press for corporate accountability in the areas of the environment, alcohol and tobacco, equal opportunity, South Africa, militarism, *maquiladoras* and other subjects. ICCR is part of a larger social/ethical investment movement which through the power of large institutional shareholders has the potential to exercise great influence in the corporate world.

*Codes on Specific Topics*

Citizen groups have initiated codes of conduct in specific arenas that are placing pressure on corporations to change their behavior. In the wake of the enormous oil spill from the *Exxon Valdez*, the Coalition for Environmentally Responsible Economies (CERES), a number of leading environmental and consumer groups, came together in 1992 to launch the CERES Principles, a list of ten principles of environmentally sustainable behavior that requires signatory firms to submit annual reports on their compliance with the principles. Firms as diverse as Ben & Jerry's and General Motors have signed on.

The Coalition for Justice in the Maquiladoras pulled together over 100 environmental, religious, community, labor, women's and Latino organizations to fight the horrendous working and environmental conditions in the over 2,000 factories that dot the 2,000-mile US-Mexico border. The Coalition drew on US, Mexican and UN standards to craft the 'Maquiladora Standards of Conduct' that spells out acceptable standards for firms in the areas of environment, health and safety, worker rights and community impact.

## MOVING FORWARD

Corporations, through their global webs, are undermining democracy around the world. They are contributing less to national welfare and increasingly divorce their concerns from national well-being. They increasingly can both escape and undermine national government policies. And, they are eroding the bonds of trust that have historically tied together communities, workers and businesses. New movements of corporate accountability can be built upon the organizations that have carried on this work for two decades combined with new groups that are taking on the corporate agenda. We are in a period of discussion, debate and strategizing that can produce new global campaigns for corporate accountability.

## NOTES

1. Calculated by the author. The combined sales of the world's top 200 firms exceeded $5 trillion in 1992, while global gross national product (GNP) was around $20 trillion.
2. See Richard J. Barnet and John Cavanagh, *Global Dreams: Imperial Corporations and the New World Order* (New York: Simon & Schuster, 1994).
3. See Sarah Anderson, John Cavanagh, Dave Ranney and Paul Schwalb (eds), *NAFTA's First Year: Lesson for the Hemisphere* (Washington, DC:

Institute for Policy Studies (IPS), 1994).

4. For other examples, see John Cavanagh, John Gershman, Karen Baker and Gretchen Helmke (eds), *Trading Freedom: How Free Trade Affects our Lives, Work and Environment* (San Francisco: Food First, and Washington, DC: Institute for Policy Studies, 1992) especially pp. 68–75.
5. Barnet and Cavanagh, *Global Dreams: Imperial Corporations and the New World Order*, pp. 319–20.
6. *Forbes*, April 25, 1994.
7. See Working Group of the Debt Crisis Network, *From Debt to Development: Alternatives to the International Debt Crisis* (Washington, DC: Institute for Policy Studies, 1986).
8. Harris Gleckman and Riva Krut, *Transnational Corporations, International Regulation and Competition Policy: The Next Arena for International Action* (Portland, ME: Benchmark Environmental Consulting, 1994).
9. John Cavanagh, Lance Compa, Allan Ebert, Bill Goold, Kathy Selvaggio and Tim Shorrock, *Trade's Hidden Costs: Worker Rights in a Changing World Economy* (Washington, DC: International Labor Rights Education and Research Fund, 1988).
10. See, for example, the August 1994 'Social Charter for Democratic Development' adopted by the Asian and Pacific Regional Organization of the International Confederation of Free Trade Unions.
11. See, for example, Martin Khor, *Why GATT and the WTO Should Not Deal With Labour Standards* (Geneva: Third World Network, 1994, mimeo, p. 1).
12. An Initiating Statement by The Alliance for Responsible Trade, Washington, DC; Citizens Trade Campaign, Washington, DC; and The Mexican Action Network on Free Trade, Mexico City.
13. For a detailed analysis, see Diane Orentlicher and Timothy Gelatt, 'Public Law, Private Actors: The Impact of Human Rights on Business Investors in China', *Northwestern Journal of International Law & Business*, vol. 14/1 (Fall 1993) pp. 66–129.
14. Mitchell Zuckoff, 'Taking a Profit and Inflicting a Cost', *Boston Globe*, July 10, 1994.
15. Orentlicher and Gelatt, 'Public Law, Private Actors: The Impact of Human Rights on Business Investors in China'.
16. Eric Kolodner, 'Transnational Corporations: Impediments or Catalysts of Social Development', Occasional Paper No. 5 for the World Summit for Social Development (Geneva: United Nations Research Institute for Social Development, November 1994) p. 29.
17. Richard Grossman and Frank Adams, *Taking Care of Business: Citizenship and the Charter of Incorporation* (Cambridge, MA: Charter Ink, 1993).
18. At least 100 suits were filed in US federal and state courts regarding the poisonous gas explosion at the Union Carbide plant in Bhopal, Bihar, India, on December 3, 1984, that killed 2,000 people and

injured 200,000 others. Most suits were filed on behalf of the Bhopal residents (as personal injury suits). In 1985, all of the federal personal injury suits were transferred to the Southern District of New York. Also in 1985, the government of India filed a lawsuit in New York's Southern District against Union Carbide on behalf of all Bhopal victims seeking compensatory and punitive damages. The suits have been resolved with a settlement in which Union Carbide paid $470 million in recompense to the victims of the gas explosion.

19. Chapter in John Cavanagh, Daphne Wysham and Marcos Arruda (eds), *Beyond Bretton Woods: Alternatives to the Global Economic Order* (London: Pluto Press; Washington, DC: Institute for Policy Studies; and Amsterdam: Transnational Institute (TNI), 1994).
20. For an inventory of consumer boycotts ongoing in the United States at any given movement, see the magazine *Co-op America Quarterly*'s 'Boycott Action News'. The list of 57 is from the Fall 1994 issue.

# Glossary

**African, Caribbean and Pacific (ACP) Countries** – Countries entitled to tariff concessions and official development assistance under the Lomé Conventions. As of 1992, roughly 65 developing countries received EC foreign aid in the form of capital investment, debt relief, duty reductions, subsidies or technical assistance. The aid package for 1996–2000 is projected to be about $15 billion.

**Agenda 21** – The main strategy document for environmentally responsible development for the twenty-first century prepared at the United Nations Conference on Environment and Development (UNCED) in Rio de Janeiro, in June 1992. The Agenda 21 action plan covers over 100 program areas, including commitments to allocate international aid to protect natural habitat and diversity and to programs with high returns for poverty alleviation and environmental health.

**Balance-of-Payments deficit/surplus** – The balance of payments consists of the current account (flows of goods and services) and the capital account (flows of financial assets). A country is said to have a balance-of-payments deficit when its income (credits from exports, cash inflows, loans, etc.) is less than its payments (debits from imports, cash outflows, debt repayments, etc.). A balance-of-payments surplus occurs when income is greater than payments.

**Bank for International Settlement (BIS)** – An intergovernmental financial institution originally established in 1930 to assist and coordinate the transfer of payments among national central banks. This contrasts with the Board of Governors of the IMF which is comprised of Ministers of Finance. The creation of the IMF constrained the subsequent expansion of the BIS's international monetary role and activities. Main current activities of the bank are to assist central banks in managing and investing their monetary reserves, and to collect and disseminate information on macroeconomic topics and international monetary affairs.

**Beggar-thy-neighbor policies** – Economic policies by one country to improve its domestic economy, but which have adverse effects on other economies, such as competitive devaluations and tariffs.

**Blair House Accord** – A 1992 agreement between the European Community and the United States on reductions in agricultural subsidies in order to complete the Uruguay Round. However, the Blair House Accord did not become effective because heavily subsidized French farmers objected to its terms.

**Bretton Woods institutions (BWIs)** – The institutions founded at the conference of Bretton Woods, New Hampshire, in 1944, that is, the World Bank and the International Monetary Fund (IMF).

**Cairns Group** – The Cairns Group is composed of 14 agricultural exporting countries, a coalition that formed in Cairns, Australia, in 1986 with the goal of pressuring the United States and the European Community to reduce agricultural subsidies.

**Concessionality** – A description of lending conditions which reduce the burden to the borrower, like a low interest rate. Concessionality should not be confused with conditionality, which is a description of requirements for borrowers to receive loans.

**Convention of Biological Diversity** – A UN convention adopted on June 5, 1992 at the United Nations Conference on Environment and Development (UNCED) in Rio de Janeiro. The Convention came into force on December 29, 1993; see also Agenda 21.

**Debt crisis** – Extreme difficulties of many developing countries to repay their loans since 1982, caused mainly by drastically increasing interest rates in the hard-currency creditor countries and a slowing world economy which led to lower exports.

**Deflation** – The opposite of inflation, that is, a sustained fall in the general price level. More generally, although incorrectly, deflation is also used as a sustained reduction of the inflation rate, that is, a lower increase in the general price level.

**Depreciation/devaluation** – A decrease in the value of a currency. If the exchange rate is defined in terms of foreign currency over domestic currency, then a devaluation of the domestic currency implies a decrease of the exchange rate. If the exchange rate is defined in terms of domestic currency over foreign currency, then a devaluation of the domestic currency implies an increase of the exchange rate.

**Development (equitable, sustainable and participatory)** – A healthy growing economy which (a) distributes the benefits widely, (b) meets the needs of the present generation without compromising the needs of future generations and (c) provides for human rights and freedoms, effective governance and increasing democratization.

**Development Committee** – Officially the 'Joint Ministerial Committee of the Boards of Governors of the World Bank and the IMF on the Transfer of Real Resources to Developing Countries'. Established in October 1974, it currently consists of 24 members, generally Ministers of Finance, appointed in turn to successive periods of two years by one of the countries or groups of countries that designates a member of the World Bank's or the IMF's Board of Executive Directors. The Committee advises and reports to the Boards of Governors of the Bank and the IMF.

**Dispute Settlement Understanding (DSU)** – Also called 'Understanding on Rules and Procedures Governing the Settlement of Disputes'. The DSU, the fourth of six main sets of WTO agreements, sets forth comprehensive rules for dispute settlement which strengthen the pre-Uruguay enforcement procedures. For example, a member can no longer object to the establishment of a panel, nor its terms of reference, nor its composition.

**Dunkel Text** – Draft Final Act of 450 pages containing 28 draft agreements was prepared in December 1991 by Arthur Dunkel, Director-General of the GATT (1980–93), following five years of inconclusive negotiations of the Uruguay Round.

**Economic and Social Council (ECOSOC)** – One of the original six major organs of the United Nations. It coordinates the economic and social work of the United Nations and the specialized agencies and institutions. The Council is charged with making recommendations and initiatives relating to all economic and social questions.

**European Bank for Reconstruction and Development (EBRD)** – Also known as the European Bank, the EBRD is a development bank created in Paris in 1990 by the European Community and other countries around the globe to finance the economic development of the former Soviet Union and Eastern European countries.

**Executive Director** – The Executive Directors represent the member governments of the World Bank. According to the Articles of Agreement, the five largest shareholders – the United States, Japan, Germany, France and the United Kingdom – each appoint one Executive Director. The other countries are grouped into 19 constituencies, each represented by an Executive Director who is elected by a country or a group of countries. The same applies to the Executive Directors of the IMF.

**Externality** – A positive or negative spillover effect from consumption or production of one economic agent to another one, based on the non-existence of markets, for example it is impossible to define and enforce property rights for clean air.

**Foreign direct investment** – Investment abroad, usually by transnational corporations, involving an element of control by the investor over the corporation in which the investment is made.

**Foreign portfolio investment** – Investment abroad, mainly in financial (including monetary) assets, whereby the investment is too small to give an investor partial or total control of a company. The sale of these assets allows the investor to back out within a short period of time.

**G-7** – Group of Seven; the seven major industrial countries (Canada, France, Italy, Germany, Japan, the United Kingdom and the United States). Since 1976, G-7 heads of government have met annually at Economic Summits to coordinate macroeconomic policies. Since 1987, G-7 summits have become mammoth media events, the earlier spirit of informal discussion has been lost, and the serious economic policymaking has shifted to the G-7 Finance Ministers' meeting, which may or may not coincide with the G-7 summits. Most recently, Russia also participates at the G-7 summits, although on an as yet undefined basis.

**G-24** – Group of 24; formed at the 1972 Lima meeting to represent the interests of the developing countries in negotiations on international monetary affairs. The Group's members are: Algeria, Argentina, Brazil, Colombia, Côte d'Ivoire, Egypt, Ethiopia, Gabon, Ghana, Guatemala, India, Iran, Lebanon, Mexico, Nigeria, Pakistan, Peru, Philippines, Sri Lanka, Syria, Trinidad and Tobago, Venezuela and Zaire. China attends as an invitee.

**General Agreement on Tariffs and Trade (GATT)** – An agreement signed by the 23 Contracting Parties of the Geneva Trade Conference of October 1947, which became effective January 1948. It set out rules of conduct, provided a forum for multilateral negotiations regarding the solution of trade problems and aimed to eliminate tariffs and other barriers to trade. With the completion of the multilateral trade agreements of the Uruguay Round in 1994, the GATT was superceded by the World Trade Organization (WTO). (See also Uruguay Round and World Trade Organization.)

**General Agreement on Trade in Services (GATS)** – The second of six main sets of agreements of the WTO, it extends the existing international regulations considerably. GATS consists of three main elements: (a) a set of general concepts, principles and rules that apply to measures affecting trade in services; (b) specific commitments that apply to service sectors listed in a party's schedule, and (c) a set of annexes that take into account sectoral specifications and allow for temporary exemptions to the most favored nation obligation.

**Generalized System of Preferences (GSP)** – Introduced in 1971, the system provides preferential access to the markets of industrial countries for some exports from developing countries.

**Gross domestic product (GDP)** – GDP is the value of all final goods and services produced in the country within a given period.

**Gross national product (GNP)** – GNP is the value of all final goods and services produced by domestically owned factors of production, whether inside or outside the national borders, within a given period.

**Havana Charter** - The charter embodied in the Final Act of the United Nations Conference on Trade and Employment held in Havana, Cuba during November 1947–March 1948, which proposed the creation of a new permanent UN agency, the International Trade Organization (ITO). Since the ITO was never ratified, the GATT became *de facto* the international organization for trade-related issues.

**Human capital** - Investments in people (human resources) to improve their productivity, especially education and job training.

**Human Development Index (HDI)** - UNDP's composite measure of human development containing indicators representing three equally weighted dimensions of human development: life expectancy at birth, adult literacy and mean years of schooling, and income per capita in purchasing power parity dollars.

**Import substitution policy** - A policy of replacing imports with domestic products, which involves charging higher import duties and/or restricting imports through quotas or outright bans.

**Inter-American Development Bank** - An international financial institution created in 1959 to help accelerate the economic and social development of its member countries in Latin America and the Caribbean. The Bank is owned by its 46 member countries; 28 regional members from the Western Hemisphere, and 18 non-regional members from Europe, Asia and the Middle East. The Bank's headquarters are in Washington, DC.

**International Bank for Reconstruction and Development (IBRD)** - Commonly referred to as the World Bank, founded in 1944 at Bretton Woods. A lending institution whose official aim is to promote long-term economic growth that reduces poverty in developing countries. See also: World Bank Group.

**International Development Association (IDA)** - An institution within the World Bank Group, established in 1960 to promote economic development in the world's poorest countries.

**International Finance Corporation (IFC)** - The World Bank Group's investment bank for developing countries, established in 1956. It lends directly to private companies and makes equity investments in them, without guarantees from governments.

**International Labour Organisation (ILO)** – Established in 1919 by the Treaty of Versailles, the ILO became a specialized agency of the United Nations in 1946. The ILO promotes international cooperation regarding policies designed to achieve full employment, improve working conditions, extend social security and raise general living standards.

**International Monetary Fund (IMF)** – Established in December 1945 following ratification of the Articles of Agreement of the Fund, formulated at the Bretton Woods conference in 1944. The Fund became a specialized agency of the United Nations in 1947 and acts as a monitor of the world's currencies by helping to maintain an orderly system of payments between all countries. To this end, it lends money to its members facing serious balance-of-payments deficits, subject to a variety of conditions.

**International Trade Organization (ITO)** – In 1947, the United Nations Economic and Social Council (ECOSOC) convened an International Conference on Trade and Development in Havana, Cuba, which drew up the Havana Charter, proposing the establishment of an International Trade Organization under the aegis of the United Nations. The ITO had been part of the original plan for the 1944 Bretton Woods conference. Although 50 countries signed the Havana Charter, it failed to receive the necessary number of ratifications and the idea of a permanent UN trade body was never realized. See also: GATT, UNCTAD and WTO.

**Lomé Convention** – A trade and economic cooperation convention signed first in 1975 at Lomé, the capital of Togo, by the European Community (EC) member countries and 46 African, Caribbean and Pacific (ACP) developing countries. The most recent Lomé Convention between the EC and ACP countries was concluded in 1989 and expires in 1999.

***Maquiladora* Program** – A program created by the Mexican government in 1966 in order to boost employment in the border zone to the United States. The program's aim is to encourage US firms to establish assembly plants in Mexico that would use relatively low-cost Mexican labor. The special exemptions given to investors constituted a substantial exception to Mexico's formerly strict foreign investment regulations.

**Mixed economy** – A system which combines competitive private enterprise with some degree of government activity. While the allocation of resources is dominated by individual actions through the price mechanism, the government plays some role in determining the level of aggregate demand by means of fiscal and monetary policy.

**Most favored nation (MFN) status** – The result of the GATT (or any other trade agreement) whereby all contracting parties guarantee to grant each other the same favorable treatments they offer to any other country. Exceptions are customs unions and free trade agreements.

**Multi-Fibre Arrangement (MFA)** – A set of complicated multilateral umbrella agreements which limits the flow of textiles and clothing produced in developing countries for sale in developed countries. The application of import quotas for textiles and clothing from developing countries, but not to those from other developed countries, is a clear breach of the GATT principles of non-discrimination. The fourth MFA began in 1986 and was scheduled to expire in 1991. However, the MFA became part of the Uruguay Round of GATT negotiations which concluded April 15, 1994, at Marrakesh (Morocco), where it was agreed to give the MFA another ten years to be phased out.

**Multilateral Investment Guarantee Agency (MIGA)** – A member of the World Bank Group, the MIGA helps to smooth the flow of foreign investment by insuring investors against non-commercial risks and providing investment advice and promotion services.

**Multilateral Trade Organization** – The original name of the World Trade Organization (WTO) during the later stage of the Uruguay Round. It was changed at the insistence of the United States in the final meeting before Marrakesh from Multilateral Trade Organization to World Trade Organization.

**Neoclassical economics** – A body of economic theory which uses the general techniques of the original nineteenth-century marginalist economists. Today, it is often combined with the liberal doctrine, which advocates the greatest possible use of markets and the forces of competition within economic activity. Thus, economic policy based on neoclassical economics is often said to use either the neoclassical or the neoliberal paradigm.

**Net flow of capital** – The difference between total flow of capital into and out of a country or institution: the net flow of capital is the gross flow of capital out minus the gross flow of capital in. For example, if the total amount of capital which flows into a country exceeds the total amount of capital which flows out of a country, the country is said to be a net creditor country. Thus the net flow of capital is positive.

**North American Free Trade Agreement (NAFTA)** – A trilateral treaty creating a free trade area between Canada, Mexico and the United States, concluded on August 12, 1992. NAFTA gradually phases out most internal trade and investment barriers. The treaty creates a mechanism for trilateral dispute settlements; includes safeguards against import surges; imposes strict domestic content in rules of origin; mandates enforcement of intellectual property rights and provides for the gradual harmonization of labor, health and environmental standards.

**Omnibus Trade and Competitiveness Act** – A 1988 US law enacted to enhance US competitiveness and improve enforcement of US trade laws. The act establishes formal procedures for monitoring foreign import barriers, provides for domestic export enhancement, authorizes retaliation for violations of US intellectual property laws and bars foreign takeovers of domestic companies in strategically vital sections.

**Organization for Economic Cooperation and Development (OECD)** – Originally set up as the Organization for European Economic Cooperation (OEEC) to coordinate Marshall Plan aid in 1948, the OECD took on its present form in 1961 in order to encourage economic growth and maintain financial stability among its 25 member countries: Australia, Austria, Belgium, Canada, Denmark, Finland, France, Germany, Greece, Iceland, Ireland, Italy, Japan, Luxemburg, Mexico, the Netherlands, New Zealand, Norway, Portugal, Spain, Sweden, Switzerland, Turkey, the United Kingdom and the United States. Mexico joined in 1994; South Korea is expected to join in late 1996 or early 1997 as the twenty-sixth member.

**Participatory development** – Development which includes a mechanism for enabling affected people to share in development projects or programs, beginning with identification all the way through to implementation and evaluation. On the national scale it implies a political system of human rights and freedoms, effective governance and increasing democratization.

**Punta del Este Declaration** – The GATT declaration of Punta del Este, Uruguay, which marked the beginning of the GATT's Uruguay Round in September 1986.

**Section 301 Laws** – A comprehensive provision of the 1974 US Trade Act authorizing broad unilateral retaliation against trading partners who engage in unfair trade practices and raise non-tariff barriers to US imports. The unilateral measures permitted under Section 301 contravene the obligation accepted by GATT members to resolve disputes through negotiated settlements.

**Special Drawing Right (SDR)** – The IMF's standard unit of account, introduced in 1969, which IMF member countries may use to settle international trade balances and debts if the member country meets a variety of conditions. The value of one SDR was originally expressed in terms of gold at 1/35th of an ounce of gold, the par value of the US dollar in 1969. In 1974, the SDR was converted to a value represented by 16 national currencies. Since 1981, the SDR is valued in a basket of the G-5 currencies.

**Structural adjustment program (SAP)** – Long-term assistance from the World Bank and other IFIs which is designed to restore equilibrium and promote economic growth. The original rationale for SAPs was that sound projects were not possible in an unsound policy environment. Thus, SAPs became a new instrument to influence macroeconomic policies of developing countries, based on neoclassical economics, advocating *laissez-faire* and free trade.

**Sustainable development** – Development which meets the needs of the present generation without compromising the needs of future generations.

**Terms of trade** – The quotient between an index of export prices and an index of import prices. When a country's terms of trade decline, as is the case for many developing countries, it is necessary to export more in order to import the same quantity of goods and services.

**Trade-Related Intellectual Property Rights (TRIPs)** – The third of the six main sets of agreements of the WTO, it extends existing international regulations considerably. TRIPs oblige governments to take positive action to protect intellectual property rights and set minimum standards for six types of intellectual property: trademarks, geographical indications, industrial designs, layout designs of integrated circuits, copyrights and patents.

**Trade-Related Investment Measures (TRIMs)** – A subsection within the first of six main sets of WTO agreements. This first main set contains agreements on trade in goods.

**Transnational corporation (TNC)** – A large enterprise having a home base in one country but operating wholly or partially-owned subsidiaries in other countries. Such corporations expand on an international scale to take advantage of economies of scale and to benefit from enjoying near-monopoly status, which power is often used against the interest of the developing countries they operate in.

**Understanding on Rules and Procedures Governing the Settlement of Disputes** – See: Dispute Settlement Understanding (DSU).

**United Nations Conference on Trade and Development (UNCTAD)** – The conference, first convened in 1964, is now a permanent organ of the UN General Assembly. All members of the United Nations or of its specialized agencies are members of the conference which has a permanent executive organ and a permanent secretariat. Its role has been to protect and champion the case of developing countries against the trade policies of the developed countries. UNCTAD's major success has been in promoting the Generalized System of Preferences (GSP).

**United Nations Development Programme (UNDP)** – Created in 1966, it combined the UN Expanded Programme of Technical Assistance and the UN Special Fund. It is responsible for administering and coordinating development projects and technical assistance provided under the auspices of or in liaison with the UN system of development agencies and organizations.

**Uruguay Round** – The eighth round of GATT negotiations, launched in September 1986 in Punta del Este (Uruguay) and concluded on April 15, 1994 at Marrakesh (Morocco). It dealt with unfinished business from earlier GATT rounds and new issues, such as trade in services, the protection of intellectual property rights, trade-related investment measures, and especially, the establishment of the World Trade Organization (WTO).

**World Bank** – See: International Bank for Reconstruction and Development.

**World Bank Group** – Consists of the International Bank for Reconstruction and Development (IBRD) (commonly referred to as the World Bank), the International Finance Corporation (IFC), the International Development Association (IDA), the International Center for Settlements of Investment Disputes (ICSID), and the Multilateral Investment Guarantee Agency (MIGA), all of them based in Washington, DC.

**World Trade Organization (WTO)** – The WTO is the successor of the GATT, after a transition period, during which all the major trading nations agree to accept the WTO. It is a procedural umbrella agreement to provide an institutional and organizational framework for the administration of the multilateral trade agreements concluded at the Uruguay Round. See also: General Agreement on Tariffs and Trade, and Uruguay Round.

# Bibliography

Abugre, Charles 'Critique of World Bank/IMF Insistence on More Structural Adjustment Policies for Least Developed Countries' in *Third World Economics* no. 74 (1993) pp. 17–20.

Addison, John T. and W. Stanley Siebert 'The Social Charter of the European Community: Evolution and Controversies' in *Industrial and Labor Relations Review*, vol. 44, no. 4 (July 1991) pp. 597–625.

Agarwal, Anil K. 'Nature and Society in Modernising India' in Borden, C.M. (ed.) *Contemporary India: Essays on the Uses of Tradition* (Delhi: Oxford University Press, 1989).

Agosin, Manuel and Diana Tussie (eds) *Trade and Growth: New Dilemmas in Trade Policy* (London: Macmillan, 1993).

Agosin, Manuel R., Diana Tussie and Gustavo Crespi 'Developing Countries and the Uruguay Round: An Evaluation and Issues for the Future' in United Nations Conference on Trade and Development (UNCTAD) *International Monetary and Financial Issues for the 1990s*, Research Papers for the Group of Twenty-Four (New York and Geneva: United Nations, 1995) pp. 1–34.

Amin, Samir *Accumulation On a World Scale* (New York: Monthly Review Press, 1974).

Anderson, Sarah, John Cavanagh, Dave Ranney and Paul Schwalb (eds) *NAFTA's First Year: Lesson for the Hemisphere* (Washington, DC: Institute for Policy Studies (IPS), 1994).

Appleyard, Dennis R. and Alfred J. Field *International Economics*, 2nd ed. (Chicago et al.: Irwin, 1995).

Bagchi, Amiya K. 'Transnational Banks, US Power Game and Global Impoverishment' in *Economic & Political Weekly*, vol. 27, no. 22 (May 30, 1992) pp. 1133–6.

Baran, Paul A. *The Political Economy of Growth* (New York: Monthly Review Press, 1957).

Barnet, Richard J. and John Cavanagh *Global Dreams: Imperial Corporations and the New World Order* (New York: Simon & Schuster, 1994).

Bhagwati, Jagdish, *The World Trading System at Risk* (Princeton, NJ: Princeton University Press, 1991).

Blank, Rebecca and Maria Hanratty 'Down and Out in North America: Recent Trends in Poverty Rates in the United States and Canada' in *Quarterly Journal of Economics*, vol. 107 (February 1992) pp. 233–54.

Card, David and Richard B. Freeman 'Small Differences That Matter: Canada vs the United States' in Freeman, Richard B. (ed.) *Working Under Different Rules*, A National Bureau of Economic Research Project Report (New York: Russell Sage Foundation, 1994) pp. 189–222.

Cavanagh, John, Lance Compa, Allan Ebert, Bill Goold, Kathy Selvaggio and Tim Shorrock *Trade's Hidden Costs: Worker Rights in a Changing World Economy* (Washington, DC: International Labor Rights Education and Research Fund, 1988).

Cavanagh, John, John Gershman, Karen Baker and Gretchen Helmke (eds), *Trading Freedom: How Free Trade Affects our Lives, Work and Environment* (San Francisco: Food First, and Washington, DC: Institute for Policy Studies, 1992).

Cavanagh, John, Daphne Wysham and Marcos Arruda (eds) *Beyond Bretton Woods: Alternatives to the Global Economic Order* (London: Pluto Press and Washington, DC: Institute for Policy Studies, and Amsterdam: Transnational Institute (TNI), 1994).

Central Bank of Sri Lanka *Annual Report* (Colombo: Central Bank of Sri Lanka, various issues).

Chakravarty, Sukhamoy *Development Planning: The Indian Experience* (Oxford: Clarendon Press, 1987).

Chandra, Nirmal K. 'The New Economic Policy, Stagnation and De-Industrialization', paper presented at a Seminar on New Economic Policy, at the Indian Institute of Management (IIM), Calcutta, August 19–21, 1993.

Chandra, Nirmal K. 'Modernisation for Export-Oriented Growth: A Critique of Recent Indian Policy' in Nirmal K. Chandra, *The Retarded Economies* (Bombay: Oxford University Press, 1988) pp. 339–80.

Chandra, Nirmal K. 'Long-Term Stagnation in the Indian Economy, 1900–75' in Nirmal K. Chandra, *The Retarded Economies* (Bombay: Oxford University Press, 1988) pp. 157–252.

Chaudhuri, Sudip *Indigenous Firms in Relation to Transnational Corporations in the Drug Industry in India*, Ph.D. thesis, Jawaharlal Nehru University (New Delhi: Jawaharlal Nehru University, 1984).

Chaudhuri, Sudip 'Regulation of the TNCs and the New Economic Policies', paper presented at a Seminar on New Economic Policy, at the Indian Institute of Management (IIM), Calcutta, August 19–21, 1993.

Chaudhuri, Sudip 'Dunkel Draft on Drug Patents: Background and Implications' in *Economic & Political Weekly*, vol. 28, no. 36 (September 4, 1993) pp. 1861–5.

Chossudovsky, Michel 'The "Third Worldisation" of Russia Under IMF Rule' in *Third World Economics*, no. 67 (1993) pp. 14–16.

Committee for the Promotion of Investment in Mexico *An Overview of the Maquiladora Industry in Mexico* (Washington, DC: Committee on Economic Development, January 1990).

Cornia, Giovanni A., Richard Jolly and Frances Stewart (eds) *Adjustment with a Human Face – Protecting the Vulnerable and Promoting Growth*, Vols I and II, A UNICEF Study (Oxford: Clarendon Press, 1987).

D'Mello, Bernard 'Third World Debt' in *Frontier*, vol. 16 (December 10, 1983), pp. 8–11.

D'Mello, Bernard *Foreign Collaboration in Public Sector Steel Industry* (Calcutta: Indian Institute of Management (IIM), mimeo, December, 1991).

Dhawan, R. and A. Vishwanathan 'A Guide to the Final GATT Treaty' in *Frontline*, vol. 11, no. 9 (May 6, 1994) pp. 123–9.

Divisekera, Sarath and B.S. Felmingham 'Sri Lankan Economic Performance and Income Distribution in Various Policy Epochs' in *The Singapore Economic Review*, vol. 34/1 (April 1989) pp. 43–9.

Dunning, John H. *Globalization, Economic Restructuring and Development: The Prebisch Lecture for 1994* (Geneva: UNCTAD, 1994).

Economic Intelligence Unit (EIU) *Country Report (on Sri Lanka)*, 4th Quarter, 1994 (London: EIU, 1994).

European Social Fund 'Social Action Programme' in *Bulletin of the Social Community*, no. 10 (1974) pp. 7–10.

Farber, Henry S. 'The Recent Decline of Unionization in the United States' in *Science*, vol. 238, no. 4829 (November 13, 1987) pp. 915–20.

Farber, Henry S. and Alan B. Krueger 'Union Membership in the United States: The Decline Continues' in National Bureau of Economic Research (NBER) Working Paper No. 4216 (Cambridge, MA: NBER, November 1992).

Frank, Andre G., Johan Galtung, Immanuel Wallerstein and

Chakravarthi Raghavan 'Overview of the Global Scene' in Nordenstreng, Kaarle and Herbert Schiller (eds) *Beyond National Sovereignty* (New Jersey: Ablex, 1993).

Freeman, Richard B. 'How Much Has De-Unionization Contributed to the Rise in Male Earnings Inequality?' in Danziger S. and P. Gottschalk (eds) *Uneven Tides: Rising Inequality in America* (New York: Russell Sage Foundation, 1992) pp. 133–63.

Fusfeld, Daniel R. 'The Market in History' in *Monthly Review*, vol. 45/1 (May 1993) pp. 1–8.

General Agreement on Tariffs and Trade (GATT) *Trends in International Trade: A Report by a Panel of Experts* (Geneva: GATT, 1958).

General Agreement on Tariffs and Trade (GATT) *Final Text of the Uruguay Round* (Bombay: World Trade Center, and New Delhi: Academy of Business Studies, 1994).

Gleckman, Harris and Riva Krut *Transnational Corporations, International Regulation and Competition Policy: The Next Arena for International Action* (Portland, ME: Benchmark Environmental Consulting, 1994).

Goodman, David, Bernardo Sorj and John Wilkinson *From Farming to Biotechnology* (New York: Basil Blackwell, 1987).

Greenaway, David 'Liberalizing Foreign Trade Through Rose-Tinted Glasses' in *Economic Journal*, vol. 103, no. 416 (January 1993) pp. 208–22.

Grossman, Richard and Frank Adams *Taking Care of Business: Citizenship and the Charter of Incorporation* (Cambridge, MA: Charter Ink, 1993).

Gulde, Anne-Marie 'Sri Lanka: Price Changes and the Poor', *IMF Working Paper* WP/91/46 (Washington, DC: IMF, May 1991).

Hawking, Stephen W. *A Brief History of Time: From the Big Bang to Black Holes* (Toronto and New York: Bantam Books, 1988).

Helleiner, Gerald K. 'Introduction' in United Nations Conference on Trade and Development (UNCTAD) *The International Monetary and Financial System: Developing Country Perspectives* (Geneva: UNCTAD, 1994) pp. 1–20.

Hoekman, Bernard M. 'Trade Laws and Institutions: Good Practices and the World Trade Organization' in *World Bank Discussion Papers*, no. 282 (Washington, DC: World Bank, 1995).

International Monetary Fund (IMF) *International Financial Statistics*, vol. 47/7 (Washington, DC: IMF, July 1994).

Jayawardena, Lal 'Market-Friendly Policies: An Appraisal' in *MARGA (Sri Lanka Centre for Development Studies) Quarterly Journal*, vol. 13/2 (1994) pp. 1–18.

Jayaweera, Swarna 'Structural Adjustment Policies, Industrial Development and Women in Sri Lanka' in Pamela Sparr (ed.) *Mortgaging Women's Lives: Feminist Critiques of Structural Adjustment* (London and New Jersey: Zed Books, 1994) pp. 96–115.

Kakwani, Nanak *Income Inequality, Welfare and Poverty in a Developing Economy with Applications to Sri Lanka*, Wider Working Papers, WP 4 (Helsinki: World Institute for Development Economics Research; and Tokyo: United Nations University, April 1986).

Keala, B.K. 'Final Dunkel Act: New Patent Regime: Myth and Reality' in *Frontline*, vol. 27 (May 6, 1994) pp. 14–16.

Kelegama, Saman and Ganeshan Wignaraja 'Trade Policy and Industrial Development in Sri Lanka' in *MARGA (Sri Lanka Centre for Development Studies) Quarterly Journal*, vol. 11/4 (1991) pp. 27–53.

Kenny, M. 'Is Biotechnology a Blessing for the Less Developed Nations?' in *Monthly Review*, vol. 34/11 (April 1993) pp. 11–19.

Keynes, John Maynard 'Letter to Lord Addison of May 1944' in John M. Keynes, *The Collected Writings of John Maynard Keynes* (Cambridge: Macmillan and Cambridge University Press, 1980) vol. XXVI, pp. 5–6.

Khan, Mohsin S., Peter J. Montiel and N.U. Haque 'Adjustment With Growth: Relating the Analytical Approaches of the IMF and the World Bank' in *Journal of Development Economics*, vol. 32 (1990) pp. 155–79.

Khanna, S. K. 'Deregulation and Competition in Indian Industry: Anatomy of Rent Seeking Behavior in the Corporate Sector', paper presented at a Seminar on New Economic Policy (Calcutta: Indian Institute of Management (IIM), August 19–21, 1993).

Khor, Martin *Why GATT and the WTO Should Not Deal with Labour Standards* (Geneva: Third World Network (mimeo), 1994).

Kolodner, Eric *Transnational Corporations: Impediments or Catalysts of Social Development*, Occasional Paper No. 5 for the World Summit for Social Development, November 1994 (Geneva: United Nations Research Institute for Social Development, 1994).

Krishnaji, N. 'The Demand Constraint: A Note on the Role of Food Grain Prices and Income Inequality' in Krishnaji, N. *Pauperising Agriculture: Studies in Agrarian Change and Demographic Structure* (Bombay: Sameesksha Trust, by Oxford University Press, 1992).

Krishnan, T.N. 'Population, Poverty and Employment in India' in *Economic & Political Weekly*, vol. 27, no. 46 (November 14, 1992) pp. 2479–97.

Krugman, Paul R. 'Increasing Returns, Monopolistic Competition, and International Trade' in *Journal of International Economics*, vol. 9/4 (November 1979) pp. 467–79.

Krugman, Paul R. 'A Model of Innovation, Technology Transfer, and the World Distribution of Income' in *Journal of Political Economy*, vol. 87/2 (April 1979) pp. 253–66.

Marshall, F. Ray 'Trade-Linked Labor Standards' in Macchiarola, Frank J. (ed.) *International Trade: The Changing Role of the United States* (New York: Academy of Political Science Press, 1990).

Martin, Will and L. Alan Winters (eds) *The Uruguay Round and the Developing Economies* (Washington, DC: World Bank, 1995).

Mishel, Lawrence and David Frankel *The State of Working America* (Washington, DC: Economic Policy Institute, 1990).

Morse, David A. *The Origins and Evolution of the I.L.O. and Its Role in the World Community* (Ithaca, NY: Cornell University, 1969).

Nafziger, W. Wayne *The Economics of Developing Countries*, 2nd ed. (Englewood Cliffs, NJ: Prentice Hall, 1990).

Nagaraj, R. 'Employment and Wages in Manufacturing Industries: Trends, Hypothesis and Evidence' in *Economic & Political Weekly*, vol. 29, no. 4 (January 22, 1994) pp. 177–86.

Orentlicher, Diane and Timothy Gelatt 'Public Law, Private Actors: The Impact of Human Rights on Business Investors in China' in *Northwestern Journal of International Law & Business*, vol. 14/1 (Fall 1993) pp. 66–129.

Pearce, David W. (ed.) *The MIT Dictionary of Modern Economics*, 4th ed. (Cambridge, Mass.: The MIT Press, 1992).

People's Union for Democratic Rights (PUDR) *Tall Chimneys, Dark Shadows: A Report on the Lives and Struggles of Workers in Bhilai* (Delhi: PUDR, June 1991).

Percy Mistry *Multilateral Debt: An Emerging Crisis?* (The Hague: Forum on Development and Debt (FONDAD), 1994).

Perez-Lopez, Jorge F. 'Worker Rights in the U.S. Omnibus Trade and Competitiveness Act' in *Labor Law Journal*, vol. 41 (April 1990) pp. 222–34.

Polak, Jaques J. 'Monetary Analysis of Income Formation and Payments Problems' in *IMF Staff Papers*, vol. 6, no. 1 (November 1957) pp. 1–50.

Polanyi, Karl *The Great Transformation: The Political and Economic Origins of Our Time* (Boston, MA: Beacon, 1944).

Raghavan, Chakravarthi *Recolonization: GATT, the Uruguay Round and the Third World* (London and Atlantic Highlands, NJ: Zed Books; and Penang, Malaysia: Third World Network, 1990).

Raghavan, Chakravarthi 'The New World Order and North-South Relations' in *Resurgence*, no. 9 (May 1991) pp. 16–20.

Raghavan, Chakravarthi 'The MTO: Promoter of World Trade or New Instrument of Oppression' in *Third World Economics*, no. 56–57 (January 1993) pp. 2–17.

Raghavan, Chakravarthi 'Overview of the Global Scene' in Nordenstreng, Kaarle and Herbert Schiller (eds) *Beyond National Sovereignty* (New Jersey: Ablex, 1993).

Rane, Wishvas 'Farmers' Rally Against GATT Proposals' in *Economic & Political Weekly*, vol. 28, no. 44 (October 30, 1993) pp. 2391–6.

Ravallion, Martin and Sisira Jayasuriya 'Liberalization and Inequality in Sri Lanka: A Comment' in *Journal of Development Economics*, vol. 28 (March 1988) pp. 247–55.

Radworth, Philip and Linda C. Reif (eds) *The Law of the WTO: Final Text of the GATT Uruguay Round Agreements, Summary, and a Fully Searchable Diskette* (New York, London and Rome: Oceana Publications, 1995).

Reserve Bank of India (RBI), Narasimhan Committee *Report of the Committee on the Financial System*; Summary reprinted in *Reserve Bank of India Bulletin*, vol. 46, no. 2 (February 1991) pp. 369–80.

Reserve Bank of India (RBI), Shah Committee *Report of the Working Group on Financial Companies*, Summary reprinted in *RBI Bulletin*, vol. 48, no. 4 (April 1993) pp. 527–90.

Ricardo, David 'On the Principles of Political Economy, and Taxation' (London: John Murray, 1817) as reprinted in Sraffa, Piero (ed.) with the collaboration of M.H. Dobb *The Works and Correspondence of David Ricardo*, Vol. I (Cambridge, England: University Press for the Royal Economic Society, 1951).

Rodrik, Dani *Getting Interventions Right: How South Korea and Taiwan Grew Rich*, Working Paper No. 4964 (Cambridge: National Bureau of Economic Research, December 1994).

Rodrik, Dani 'Developing Countries after the Uruguay Round' in United Nations Conference on Trade and Development (UNCTAD) *International Monetary and Financial Issues for the 1990s*, Research Papers for the Group of Twenty-Four (New York and Geneva: United Nations, 1995) pp. 35–60.

Sahai, Suman 'Patenting of Life Forms: What Does it Imply' in *Economic & Political Weekly*, vol. 29, no. 17 (April 9, 1992) pp. 878–9.

Sahai, Suman 'GATT and Patenting of Micro Organisms' in *Economic & Political Weekly*, vol. 29, no. 15 (April 9, 1994) pp. 841–2.

Sarkar, Prahirjit 'India's Balance of Payments and Exchange Rate Behavior Since 1971' in *Economic & Political Weekly*, vol. 29, no. 1 & 2 (January 1–8, 1994) pp. 43–8.

Shetty, S.L. 'Investment in Agriculture: Brief Review of Recent Trends' in *Economic & Political Weekly*, vol. 25, no. 7 & 8 (February 17–24, 1990) pp. 389–98.

Shiva, Vandana 'Farmers' Rights, Biodiversity and International Treaties' in *Economic & Political Weekly*, vol. 28, no. 14 (April 3, 1993) pp. 555–60.

Shukla, S.P. 'Resisting the World Trade Organisation: Agenda for Marrakesh' in *Economic & Political Weekly*, vol. 29, no. 11 (March 12, 1994) pp. 589–92.

Sleigh, Stephen R. (ed.) *Economic Restructuring and Emerging Patterns of Industrial Relations* (Kalamazoo, MI: Upjohn Institute, 1993).

Singer, Hans W. 'Rethinking Bretton Woods: From an Historical Perspective' in Griesgraber, Jo Marie and Bernhard G. Gunter (eds) *Promoting Development: Effective Global Institutions for the Twenty-first Century* (London: Pluto Press with Center of Concern, 1995).

Silvia, Stephen J. 'The Social Charter of the European Community: A Defeat For European Labor' in *Industrial and Labor Relations Review*, vol. 44, no. 4, (July 1991) pp. 626–43.

Sleigh, Stephen *The International Labor Organization and the Global Economy* (New York: UNA-USA Publications, 1991).

Smith, Adam *An Inquiry into the Nature and Causes of the Wealth of Nations* (London: W. Strahn and T. Cadwell, 1776; reprinted London: J.M. Dent and Sons, 1977).

Sutherland, Peter 'Success' in *GATT Focus Newsletter*, no. 104 (1993) pp. 1–4.

Sutherland, Peter 'Global Trade – the Next Challenge' in *GATT Focus Newsletter*, no. 105 (1994) pp. 5–6.

Swaminathan, Monkombu S. 'Biotechnology and Third World Agriculture' in *Science*, no. 218 (December 3, 1982) pp. 967–72.

Szecsi, Maria 'Looking Back on the Great Transformation' in *Monthly Review*, vol. 30 (January 1979) pp. 34–45.

United Nations Conference on Trade and Development (UNCTAD) *The Exchange Rate System, International Monetary and Financial Issues for Developing Countries* (Geneva: UNCTAD, 1987).

United Nations Conference on Trade and Development (UNCTAD) *Trade and Development Report 1993* (New York: United Nations, 1993).

United Nations Conference on Trade and Development (UNCTAD) *International Monetary and Financial Issues for the 1990s: Research Papers for the Group of Twenty-Four*, Vols I to VI (New York: United Nations, 1993–95).

United Nations Development Programme (UNDP) *Human Development Report* (New York: Oxford University Press, various issues).

United Nations Economic Commission for Africa (UNECA) *African Alternative Framework to Structural Adjustment Programme for Socio-Economic Recovery and Transformation* (Addis Ababa: UNECA, 1989).

United Nations International Children's Emergency Fund (UNICEF) *State of the World's Children* (Oxford et al.: Oxford University Press, published for UNICEF, various issues).

United States International Trade Commission (USITC) *The Likely Impact on the United States of a Free Trade Agreement With Mexico*, Publication 2353 (Washington, DC: USITC, 1991).

United States Office of the U.S. Trade Representative *Uruguay Round of Multilateral Trade Negotiations General Agreement on Tariffs and Trade* (Washington, DC: Government Printing Office, 1994).

Vernon, Raymond and Debora L. Spar *Beyond Globalism: Remaking American Foreign Economic Policy* (New York: The Free Press, 1989).

Weston, Ann 'The Uruguay Round: Unravelling the Implications for the Least Developed and Low-Income Countries' in United Nations Conference on Trade and Development (UNCTAD) *International Monetary and Financial Issues for the 1990s*, Research Papers for the Group of Twenty-Four (New York and Geneva: United Nations, 1995) pp. 61–98.

Working Group of the Debt Crisis Network *From Debt to Devel-*

*opment: Alternatives to the International Debt Crisis* (Washington, DC: Institute for Policy Studies, 1986).

World Bank *World Debt Tables* (Washington, DC: World Bank, 1992).

World Bank *World Development Report* (New York: Oxford University Press, various issues).

# Notes on Editors and Contributors

**Jo Marie Griesgraber** is Project Director for the Rethinking Bretton Woods project at the Center of Concern where she has worked on issues related to Third World debt and global economic justice since 1989. She holds a Ph.D. in Political Science from Georgetown University. Her most recent publications include contributions to Lowell S. Gustafson (ed.), *Economic Development Under Democratic Regimes: Neoliberalism in Latin America* (Westport, CT: Praeger, 1994) and 'In Quest of Systemic Hope: Rethinking Bretton Woods' in *Theology & Public Policy*, vol. 4, no. 2 (Washington, DC: Churches' Center for Theology and Public Policy, Winter 1994) pp. 19–33.

**Bernhard G. Gunter** has worked with the Rethinking Bretton Woods project as an intern at the Center of Concern. He is a Ph.D. candidate in Economics at The American University, Washington, DC, a member of Pax Christi, Germany, and has focused on global justice since 1980. His most recent publication is 'Financial Crises and the Great Depression in Germany, 1927–1933: A Review With Some New Facts and Arguments' in *Essays in Economic and Business History*, vol. 13 (1995) pp. 55–70.

**Tissa Balasuriya, OMI**, one of Asia's foremost Christian theologians, is International Secretary at the International Forum of Religious For Global Solidarity (IFRGS) in Sri Lanka. He holds degrees in agricultural economics from Oxford University, and in theology from the Gregorian University in Rome and the University of Paris. He was president of the Aquinas University College in Sri Lanka and is now at the Centre for Society and Religion in Colombo, Sri Lanka. His numerous articles have appeared in the United States, England, France, Spain and his native Sri Lanka.

He is author of *The Eucharist and Human Liberation* (Maryknoll, NY: Orbis Books, 1979) and of *Planetary Theology* (Maryknoll, NY: Orbis Books, 1984).

**John Cavanagh** is the co-director of the World Economy Program at the Institute for Policy Studies, and has been a Fellow of the Institute since 1983. Prior to coming to IPS, Cavanagh worked as an international economist at the United Nations Conference on Trade and Development (1977–81) and at the World Health Organization. He holds a Master's degree in Public Affairs from Princeton University and BA from Dartmouth College. He has travelled extensively in the Philippines and is an expert on Philippine social and economic issues. He has written widely in the fields of trade, debt, development and other world economy issues. Cavanagh is co-author of eight books, the latest one is *Global Dreams: Imperial Corporations and the New World Order* (New York: Simon & Schuster, 1994), a joint effort with Richard J. Barnet that examines the new age of globalization and its impact on our lives, work and environment. He also recently co-edited (with Daphne Wysham and Marcos Arruda) *Beyond Bretton Woods: Alternatives to the Global Economic Order* (London: Pluto Press; Washington, DC: Institute for Policy Studies; and Amsterdam: Transnational Institute (TNI), 1994). His articles have appeared in *Foreign Policy, New York Times, Los Angeles Times, The Nation* and other publications.

**Bernard D'Mello** is presently on the economics faculty of the Management Development Institute, Gurgaon, India. During the last 20 years he has made a livelihood in a diverse set of occupations – metallurgical engineer, working journalist, writer and columnist, and an academic economist. His concerns include the study of technology from a radical social science perspective, poverty and inequality studies, and the struggle for democratic rights. He cherishes having had the opportunity to work for and to continue his association with the *Economic and Political Weekly*, Bombay; *Frontier*, Calcutta; the Committee for the Protection of Democratic Rights, Bombay, and the People's Union for Democratic Rights, Delhi.

**Chakravarthi Raghavan** is a senior journalist/analyst from India and is the Chief Editor of the *South-North Development Monitor – SUNS*, a daily newsletter published from Geneva; Co-Editor of *Third World Economics*, Penang, Malaysia; and Geneva Representative of the Third World Network. He has been closely monitoring and analyzing the trade, environment and development scene in Geneva and the North–South negotiations. From 1947–76, he held various positions in the Indian news agency, Press Trust of India, of which he was Editor-in-Chief 1971–76. His publications include *Recolonization: GATT, the Uruguay Round and the Third World*, (London and Atlantic Highlands, NJ: Zed Books; and Penang, Malaysia: Third World Network, 1990); 'Overview of the Global Scene', in Kaarle Nordenstreng and Herbert Schiller (eds) *Beyond National Sovereignty* (New Jersey: Ablex, 1993); and many articles in academic journals.

**Stephen R. Sleigh** is the Director of Strategic Resources for the International Association of Machinists and Aerospace Workers. Prior to joining the Machinists in the fall of 1994, Dr Sleigh was the Director of Research for the Teamsters union from 1992 to 1994. He was also the Deputy Director at the Center for Labor-Management Policy Studies, City University of New York and directed the research activities of the Economic Policy Council at the United Nations Association in New York, from 1988 to 1992. Dr Sleigh earned his Ph.D. in Sociology from the City University of New York in 1991, a Master's degree in Public Administration from Harvard University's Kennedy School of Government in 1987, and a Bachelor's degree in Labor Relations from the University of Massachusetts, Amherst, in 1986. Before returning to school in 1985, Dr Sleigh worked as a printing press erector and machinist for eleven years, work which took him to seven countries and over fifty newspapers over a seven-year period. In addition to publishing numerous articles and reports, Dr Sleigh has edited *Economic Restructuring and Emerging Patterns of Industrial Relations* (Kalamazoo, MI: Upjohn Institute, 1993).

# Rethinking Bretton Woods

## PROJECT SPONSORS

* Personal Capacity, organization listed for identification only.

**Charles Abugre**
Third World Network
GHANA

**Adebayo Adedeji**
African Centre for Development and Strategic Studies
NIGERIA

**Peggy Antrobus**
Development Alternatives with Women for a New Era (DAWN)
BARBADOS

**Tissa Balasuriya, OMI**
Centre for Society and Religion
SRI LANKA

**David Barkin** *
Lincoln Institute of Land Policy
Cambridge, MA and MEXICO

**Leonor Briones**
Freedom from Debt Coalition
PHILIPPINES

**Edward Broadbent and David Gillies**
International Centre for Human Rights and Democratic Development
CANADA

**Salvie D. Colina**
Asian Center for the Progress of Peoples
HONG KONG

**Sarath Fernando**
Devasarana Development Centre
SRI LANKA

**Susan Fleck and Bernhard Gunter**
Economics Graduate Student Union
The American University
Washington, DC USA

**Louis Goodman**
Dean, School of International Service
The American University
Washington, DC USA

**J. Bryan Hehir** *
Harvard University
Cambridge, MA USA

**Gabriel Izquierdo, SJ**
Centro de Investigación y Educación Popular (CINEP)
COLOMBIA

**Fatima Mello**
Federation of Organizations for Social and
Educational Assistance (FASE)
BRAZIL

**Guy Mhone**
Southern Africa Regional Institute for Policy Studies
ZIMBABWE

**Luis Peirano and Humberto Campodónico**
Centro de Estudios y Promoción del Desarrollo (DESCO)
PERU

**Sebasti L. Raj, SJ**
Indian Social Institute
INDIA

**Jorge Sabato** *
Centro de Estudios Avanzados
ARGENTINA

**Francisco Sagasti**
Grupo de Análisis para el Desarrollo (GRADE)
PERU

**Tom Schlesinger**
Southern Finance Project
Philomont, VA USA

**Kavaljit Singh**
Public Interest Research Group
INDIA

**Rob van Drimmelen**
World Council of Churches
SWITZERLAND

**Peter van Tuijl and Augustinus Rumansara**
International NGO Forum on Indonesian Development
INDONESIA / THE NETHERLANDS

**Layashi Yaker**
United Nations Economic Commission for Africa
ETHIOPIA

**Noel Keizo Yamada, SJ**
Sophia University
JAPAN

## PROJECT ADVISORY GROUP

**Nii Akwuettah**
Africa Development Foundation

**Nancy Alexander**
Bread for the World Institute

**Steven Arnold**
Professor, School of International Service
The American University

Ambassador **Richard Bernal**
Embassy of Jamaica

**Daniel Bradlow**
Professor, Washington College of Law
The American University

**Robert Browne**
Economic Consultant

**Margaret Crahan**
Luce Professor of Religion, Power and Political Process
Occidental College, Los Angeles

**Maria Floro**
Professor, Department of Economics
The American University

**Louis Goodman**
Dean, School of International Service
The American University

**Jo Marie Griesgraber**
Project Director, Center of Concern

**Chandra Hardy**
International Development Training Institution

**James E. Hug, SJ**
Director, Center of Concern

**Constantine Michalopoulos**
The World Bank

**Moisés Naím**
Senior Fellow, Carnegie Endowment for International Peace

Ambassador **Margaret Taylor**
Embassy of Papua New Guinea

**Marijke Torfs**
Friends of the Earth/USA

# Index

Note: For acronyms see list on pp.xi-xii.
**Bold** page numbers refer to Tables and Figures.
*Italic* page numbers refer to the Glossary.

*Index by Auriol Griffith-Jones*